ELITE S

EDITOR: MART

Inside the Soviet Army Today

Text by STEVEN J. ZALOGA

Colour plates by RON VOLSTAD

OSPREY PUBLISHING LONDON

Published in 1987 by
Osprey Publishing Ltd
Member company of the George Philip Group
12–14 Long Acre, London WC2E 9LP
© Copyright 1987 Osprey Publishing Ltd

British Library Cataloguing in Publication Data

Zaloga, Steven J.
  Inside the Soviet army today.—(Elite series; 12)
  1. Union of Soviet Socialist Republics, *Armiia*
  I. Title   II. Series
  355'.00947   UA772

  ISBN 0-85045-741-6

Filmset in Great Britain
Printed through Bookbuilders Ltd, Hong Kong

Author's note

The Soviet Army has been the subject of dozens of
books over the past decade covering many aspects of
its history, organisation, equipment and doctrine.
Rather than present a thin rehashing of well-covered
subjects, the aim in this short monograph is to look at
the Soviet Army from an 'ant's-eye' view. The focus
of this book is the daily experiences of a young recruit
in today's Soviet Army. The author would like to
thank many friends who have made this book
possible, especially for their help in providing much of
the new information on Soviet uniforms. Jim Loop
and Gordon Rottman provided considerable help on
recent Soviet uniform changes in Afghanistan. Beryl
Barnett Jr. provided many excellent photos of
equipment from his collection, which were used in the
preparation of the plates. David Isby provided some
unique documents relating to Soviet troops in
Afghanistan. Paul Cardin interviewed a number of
ex-Soviet servicemen regarding their experiences. Vika
Edwards of Sovfoto helped in locating many of the
photos used here. Kira Caiafa of Victor Kamkin Inc.
was very helpful in obtaining Soviet publications.
Finally, a note of thanks to the many ex-Soviet Army
emigrés who have patiently answered my questions
over the years. For readers interested in Soviet troops
in Afghanistan, or Soviet élite forces such as the
VDV, more detailed coverage can be found in other
books in Osprey's Elite 5, *Soviet Bloc Elite Forces*, and
MAA178, *Russia's War in Afghanistan*.

Artist's note

Pre-Service Indoctrination

'Military service is the sacred obligation of Soviet citizens'; so reads the Constitution of the USSR. For a young Soviet man, the chances are very great that he will be obliged to serve for at least two years in one branch or another of the Soviet Armed Forces.

By the time that they reach the conscription age of 18 years, most Soviet boys will already be far more familiar with military life than their counterparts in Western Europe or America. Soviet society is far more militarised than most other European societies, even compared with the other Warsaw Pact countries. The exploits of the Soviet Armed Forces during the Second World War—better known as the *Great Patriotic War* in the USSR—are recounted daily on television and radio and in the print media. It is rare to find a bookstore without a shelf devoted to war stories, or to read a magazine aimed at young adults which does not contain such material. In some areas it has become a Soviet tradition to lay flowers at a war memorial following wedding ceremonies. Members of the Young Pioneers, the state youth movement for pre-teenagers, serve as guards of honour at local war memorials, bedecked in special uniforms and often carrying weapons. This fixation on the war stems, in part, from the enormous human cost of the fighting—nearly one in ten Soviet citizens were killed between 1941 and 1945.

Other countries, such as Poland and Yugoslavia, suffered similar or greater levels of human and physical loss without a consequent militarisation of their societies. But in the Soviet Union the state's Marxist-Leninist ideology has grown stale and unattractive to the young, and fostering a romantic image of past martial glories and national heroism serves as an alternative, helping to create among the young a more traditional feeling of national loyalty

'Eyes left, Cadet Ivanov!' Cadets of one of the eight élite Suvorov Military Schools at marching drill. The schools, which provide the cream of the Soviet officer corps, have a special black cadet uniform enlivened here by red Motor Rifle branch arm patch, and red collar and shoulder insignia. (Sovfoto)

than any promoted by artificial appeals to a phony 'socialist internationalism'.

A less subtle approach to the militarisation of the young is revealed by universal military training. The 1967 changes to the Soviet constitution included the addition of mandatory and universal pre-induction military training. There are two main agencies for sponsoring pre-induction military training: state youth movements, and the school system. The Young Pioneer movement is in some ways similar to the Boy Scouts and Girl Scouts in Britain and the US, but is state sponsored, and includes a hefty dose of political and military indoctrination. Soviet children belong first to the Octobrist youth group until the age of nine when they can graduate to the Young Pioneers. Bright children, and those with sports skills or leadership qualities, are pressured to join, since the Young Pioneers is one of the main avenues of later recruitment into the Communist Party. The Young Pioneer movement fosters martial tradition by ceremony, like the guard of honour duties mentioned above, and through proselytisation. Books, comics and television programmes aimed at the Young Pioneers create a heroic image of military service. The Soviet government organises summer youth camps, both for members of the Young Pioneers, and for other young students, which usually include a military aspect. Many of the camps sponsor military training in the form of the *Zarnitsa* (Summer Lightning) war games. The camps are visited by local military personnel, together with a few armoured vehicles, and mock wargames are performed with the children brandishing unloaded rifles. These activities are 'understandably' very popular among the small

boys and often provide far more excitement than the unappealing and regimented activity otherwise offered by the summer camps.

Young Pioneers, at the age of 14, transfer to the *VLKSM* (All-Union Leninist Communist Union for the Young), better known as the Komsomol. The Komsomol movement is a very important element in state indoctrination for conscripts, since young men remain in the movement during their military duty. As in the Young Pioneer summer camps, the Komsomol sponsors similar summer wargames, called *Orlyonok* (Eaglet). These exercises are closer to real military training, and involve squad, platoon and company drills as well as preliminary weapons training. The camps familiarise young students with Soviet Army equipment and basic drill. Although this may sound pretty dull, much of the training is conducted as sport: for example, classes to familiarise Komosmol members with military communications usually involve radio direction-finding contests with teams assigned to locate a hidden transmitter.

Besides the military training offered through youth groups, all Soviet students, both boys and

'Welcome to the Army, Comrades . . .' Col. A. Sivoborod welcomes young draftees at the Kalinin Military Commissariat outside Moscow. (Sovfoto)

girls, receive military training at school during the ninth and tenth grades as a part of the NVP programme. NVP was introduced under the 1967 changes, when the basic duty term for conscript soldiers was reduced from three to two years. It was hoped that the schooling would act as a partial substitute for the year deleted from the draft duty. Even though girls are not currently drafted, their inclusion in the programme is presumably based on the assumption that they would be drafted in time of war, as they were during the Second World War.

The actual level of military training, and its content, vary enormously from region to region. The situation was so bad prior to 1977 that new guidelines had to be laid down to formalise schooling requirements. The ideal facilities for a school include a military office where the classes can be conducted, a weapons room for storing training weapons, a firing range, a drill field, an obstacle course, a sentry post and an anti-radiation shelter. By 1982 most schools had the military classroom and weapons storage room, but half of them lacked a firing range and only a quarter had the full

Private V. Sobolev receives his AK-74 rifle from Sr.Lt. V. Tsapko at the outset of his four weeks' basic training in the Siberian Military District, 1980. Sobolev wears the standard olive Field Dress with *pilotka* sidecap. (Sovfoto)

training range. There have also been problems in finding qualified teachers—known as *voyenruks*. Ideally, the *voyenruk* is a reserve military officer with higher military training and some teaching skills. In some of the more backward areas, such as in Central Asia, former officers and reserve officers are in such a demand that *voyenruks* have to be recruited from the ranks of reserve NCOs. However, most reserve NCOs in the USSR are not professional soldiers and have received very little higher military training or command experience during their brief two-year duty stint. Part of the problem is that many smaller schools do not have enough students to justify a full time *voyenruk*.

The NVP curriculum consists of 70 hours of annual training for students in grade nine and grade ten. Young men who leave school before reaching this age are given the same basic course at training points located in civilian factories. The

5

basic curriculum and the number of hours devoted to these subjects is listed below. It will be noted that boys receive more training in weapons and drill, while girls are given more training in first aid. This is in part due to traditional sexual stereotyping in Soviet society; the majority of doctors are women.

Separate from the Komsomol and the school system is the DOSAAF (Voluntary Society for Co-operation with the Army, Air Force and Navy). DOSAAF is a governmental organisation directed by the Ministry of Defence to support youth activities of interest to the Soviet Armed Forces. Probably the most familiar aspect of DOSAAF to Soviet young men is its sponsorship of sporting clubs. In the European sections of the USSR, DOSAAF sponsors three especially popular types of facility: flying clubs, sky-diving clubs and marksmanship/hunting clubs. The flying clubs provide pre-induction military training through classes on basic navigation, flying, instrument reading, and communications. Club members are taught on sailplanes, and military training aircraft ranging from primary trainers like the Yak-18, through to advanced trainers like the L-29 Delfin jet. The DOSAAF-sponsored flying clubs are the primary source of recruitment for pilots for the Soviet Air Forces and PVO. The sky-diving clubs use military-type aircraft, usually beginning with the An-2; and these clubs are the primary source of recruitment for paratroopers of the VDV Airborne Assault Force. Paratroopers of the VDV still wear their DOSAAF jump qualification badges when in the service. The DOSAAF marksmanship clubs are intended to foster basic rifle and pistol skills, and the club members are familiarised with military as well as sporting weapons.

In more backward rural regions of the USSR, DOSAAF sponsors motoring clubs. Since there are so few private cars in the USSR, these clubs serve to teach basic driving skills, as well as basic automotive repair. DOSAAF also sponsors more conventional sports clubs, as leadership in sports is regarded as a good indicator of leadership ability in the army.

The bane of recruits the world over—marching drill. These young draftees are put through their paces by Lt. I. Gareyev, who wears Everyday Dress/On Duty. Due to the Soviet forces' lack of a professional NCO class, lieutenants carry out many of the duties undertaken by senior NCOs in Western armies. (Sovfoto)

Basic Military Training (hours)

Subject	Grade 9		Grade 10	
	boys	girls	boys	girls
Introduction	I	I	—	—
The Soviet Armed Forces in the Defence of the Motherland	4	4	7	7
Armed Forces Regulations	3	3	7	—
Weapon training	20	13	6	6
Tactical training	4	4	6	—
Drill training	7	—	4	—
Military Topography	—	—	2	—
Medical training	2	—	—	—
Civil Defence	29	29	—	—
Technical training	—	—	35	35
First Aid	—	16	—	19
Exams	—	—	3	3
Total hours	*70*	*70*	*70*	*70*

Besides this, the national sports effort is closely tied to the military since professional sportsmen can retain their 'amateur' standing while on active duty. Activity in DOSAAF is noted on the induction records of young men, and affects their potential selection as NCO or officer candidates.

Every year, between January and March, all 17-year-old young men are required to register for conscription at their local *voyenkomat* (military commissariat). This begins the process of conscription. The local *voyenkomat* sets up a file on all potential conscripts with the aim of helping the services select new recruits. The files will contain information on the recruit's educational background, leadership skills, family background, ethnic origins, educational plans, political background and special skills. All of these considerations are important, since each of the services has its own requirements as far as recruits are concerned.

The Ethnic Factor

The Soviet Army is the last of the great imperial armies of Europe, with soldiers from over a hundred ethnic groups speaking dozens of different and unrelated languages. Ethnicity is a major factor in Soviet society, particularly when it comes to matters of national security. The Tsarist Army avoided problems associated with recruiting from such a multi-ethnic pool by greatly limiting the intake of non-Slavic ethnic groups into its ranks. But like most mass armies of today, the Soviet Army is obliged to draw recruits from all its nationalities.

The dominant ethnic group in the USSR are the Russians. The Russians control the political and military apparatus of the country, and the only non-Russians in positions of authority have become thoroughly assimilated into Russian society. The Russians harbour suspicions about the loyalty of many of the other ethnic groups of the USSR, especially after the experiences of the Red Army in the Second World War. During the war the Germans managed to recruit a significant number of anti-Soviet units from the ranks of Soviet prisoners of war, most notably among the Ukrainians, the Cossacks and some of the Turkic-Moslem nationalities of the southern USSR. In spite of these problems, it is interesting to note that from 1942 until the middle of 1944 the Red Army was made up of 30–36 per cent non-Russians, and

Maj.Gen. S. Teteryatnikov, deputy chief of the political administration of the Soviet Central Group of Forces in Czechoslovakia, presents a senior sergeant with a diploma recognising him as an 'Exemplary Soldier', awarded—with a small medal—for outstanding performance, usually during wargames or field tests. It is prized by many soldiers, since it is entered in their service record and in their subsequent employment dossier. (Eastfoto)

that by the summer of 1944 48 per cent of the infantry were non-Russian.

Besides the matter of loyalty, ethnicity is an important factor in recruitment because of the disparate levels of economic and social development of the Soviet people. The Slavic regions of the European USSR tend to produce populations better educated and better trained in technical skills than the peoples of Central Asia and the Far East. The language of the Soviet Army is Russian, and the other Slavic peoples of the USSR are more apt to speak fluent Russian than the non-Slavic peoples. The rôle an educated, urban Ukrainian student with vocational or scientific training can play in the Army is very different from that open to the young son of a nomadic tribesman from one of the small Siberian ethnic groups.

The Soviet Union has over 100 ethnic groups and as many languages. The Russians are the largest and most dominant group, and constitute over half of the population of the USSR—about 142 million out of a total Soviet population of 275 million (in 1985). Besides the Russians, there are a number of other Slavic ethnic groups who speak languages

Future Air Assault Force officers learn their trade on simulators at the Ryazan Higher Airborne Command School. To cut costs the Soviet Army tends to use simulators more extensively than is the case in NATO. The small simulator desks mimic the commander's position in the BMD airborne assault vehicle; behind them are full-size BMD simulators, which use the same sub-scale terrain model. (Sovfoto)

related to Russian and who share a similar cultural background. The most significant of these are the Ukrainians and the Byelorussians (also called White Russians). The Ukrainians are the second largest Slavic group, numbering about 43 million. Soviet military leaders generally distinguish between the East Ukrainians and the West Ukrainians, the distinction being historical and cultural. The western portions of the Ukraine were historically under Polish dominion until the 18th century, when they fell under Austro-Hungarian control. In 1919–20 the western Ukraine returned to Poland after a short-lived attempt at national independence. This section of the Ukraine did not come under Russian control until September 1939. In terms of culture, religion and economy, this region has more in common with its Central European neighbours than with Russia. The western Ukraine has traditionally been the seat of the most vigorous elements of the Ukrainian nationalist movement, and was the wellspring both

of Ukrainian nationalist partisan forces (UPA) in 1942–49, and of Ukrainian attempts to form a national army under the Germans in 1943–45. A bloody civil war was waged in the Ukraine in 1944–49 between the nationalist UPA and Soviet forces. For this reason, the loyalty of western Ukrainians is regarded as somewhat suspect. In contrast, the eastern Ukraine has traditionally been under Russian dominion. Eastern Ukrainian cities are of mixed population, both Russian and Ukrainian, and the urban culture is heavily Russified. They play a noticeable rôle in the Soviet Army, and their loyalty to the state is regarded as second only to that of the Russians.

The Byelorussians are another Slavic group akin to the Russians, numbering about ten million. The Byelorussians have never had as vigorous a nationalist movement as the Ukrainians, and their status in the USSR is close to that of the eastern Ukrainians. The three main Slavic groups—the Russians, Ukrainians and Byelorussians—together make up the majority of Soviet citizens; about 195 million out of 276 million. There is a small Polish population in the USSR, much of it located on the western frontiers in former Polish lands, but some in Siberia due to the massive deportations of Poles from the former eastern Poland in 1940 after its conquest by the USSR. Poles who retain their national language and customs are viewed with extreme suspicion by Soviet military authorities, and are likely to be regarded as security risks.

The next largest ethnic grouping in the USSR are Muslim-Turkic peoples of Central Asia. Some of these groups share some kinship with neighbouring groups, but they are by no means a homogenous population. The Muslim-Turkic peoples number about 53 million, among whom the largest ethnic groups are the Uzbeks (15 million), Kazakhs (7.5 million), Azeris and Tatars (about 6.5 million each). Russian attitudes to the Muslim-Turkic people vary. Some groups, like the Tatars, are viewed with considerable suspicion owing to their collaboration with the Germans in the Second World War. In general, the Muslim-Turkic ethnic groups are regarded as less suitable soldiers than the Slavs due to their lower level of assimilation into Russian society, their persistent clinging to tradition and religion, and their backward economic and educational roots. The Muslim-Turkic peoples suffer from a fair amount of discrimination in the Army, and are stereotyped in Russian culture as being lazy and backward. This view is not unanimous amongst Russian army officers, however. Some officers who have commanded Central Asian troops find them hardier and less demanding than Slavs, and feel that many of them would perform particularly well in wartime in the ranks of the infantry and tank forces. Inevitably, the Ground Forces cannot fill their ranks with Slavic conscripts, and so a proportion of the combat ranks are filled out with Central Asian troops. However, Slavic troops are always in the majority in combat units of the Ground Forces, due to concern over unit reliability.

Besides the Muslim-Turkic peoples there are a variety of other ethnic minorities, including Asian groups from Siberia, and western cultures like the Moldavians and the Baltic nationalities of Lithuania, Latvia and Estonia. The Asians are regarded in much the same way as Central Asians, in that they are not well enough assimilated to be fully trusted, and the Moldavians and Balts are also regarded with some suspicion. However, these western nationalities tend to be accepted into certain technical services, as they are generally better educated than the average Soviet citizen. The largest groups besides these are the peoples of the Caucasus, notably the Armenians and Georgians, numbering 4.6 million and 3.8 million respectively. Neither group is particularly highly regarded by Soviet military authorities, due in no small measure to popular Russian preconceptions of the political and economic cultures of these two hardy peoples. The Georgians, in particular, are legendary for the rôle played by *blat* (bribes) in expediting matters in the Georgian Republic compared with the rest of the stiflingly bureaucratic Soviet state. The Soviet Army is particularly unamused by the habit of obtaining conscription deferments by bribery in these southern republics. The popular Russian stereotype of the Armenians and Georgians hints that the prosperity in these

Field training for a Motor Rifle Regiment of the Rezhitskaya Guards Motor Rifle Division ('Panfilov') in September 1981. Soviet MR Divs. have two MR Regts. equipped with BTR-60/70/80 series wheeled armoured personnel carriers, and one regiment with the BMP-1 or -2 tracked infantry fighting vehicle—as here. (Sovfoto)

Beside a BM-21 *Grad* multiple rocket launcher, troops are photographed during the *Zapad-81* exercises conducted in that year on Poland's eastern border. The soldier at left wears Airborne insignia; the others, from the Artillery and Rocket Force, are probably the crew of the BM-21. Note Model 40 helmet with alternative chin strap; officers' subdued Field collar tabs, and enlisted mens' Everyday/Field collar tabs, without metal trim, and shoulder boards. (Sovfoto)

regions has more than a little to do with their nonchalant view of the Soviet legal system. While there is some discrimination against Armenians and Georgians in the Soviet Army today, however, this was not always the case. The Red Army of the Second World War enjoyed the services of many excellent Armenian officers (such as the well-known tank commander Gen. I. Bagramian) and weapon designers (such as A.I. Mikoyan of MiG fame).

Two other ethnic minorities are rated even lower on the reliability scale: the Jews, and the Volga Germans. In spite of the prominent rôle that Jews played in the Red Army during both the Civil War and the Second World War, Russian anti-semitism and Zionist sentiment in parts of the Russian Jewish community have led to suspicion over Jewish loyalties; and the Volga Germans are distrusted simply because they are Germans.

Choosing a Service

Unlike citizens of Western Europe or North America, young Soviets are given very little leeway in selecting the service they will serve in. (Though obviously an ambitious and astute young Soviet desiring a career in the Air Force can unofficially help his chances by belonging to a DOSAAF aviation club, and a member of a DOSAAF parachuting club has a better than average chance of getting a posting to the VDV Air Assault Force.) In order to understand the recruiting process better, it is worth taking a brief look at the basic organisation of the Soviet Armed Forces, and the opportunities open to young Soviet men, depending upon their educational and ethnic backgrounds.

The Soviet Armed Forces

The Soviet Armed Forces (VS-SSSR) consist of five services, plus a variety of associated organisations. The five services of the VS-SSSR are the Strategic Missile Forces (RVSN), the Ground Forces (SV), the Air Defence Forces (PVO), the Air Forces (VVS) and the Naval Forces (VMF). As a matter of tradition, the first four services constitute the Soviet Army (*Sovietskaya Armiya*) even though all these services are administratively independent. One of the few visible manifestations of this tradition lies in uniforms, with the services of the Soviet Army following one uniform dress code, and the Navy following another. The Soviet Army was called the Red Army of Peasants and Workers (RKKA) prior to 1947.

Besides these services, the Ministry of Defence also controls about a dozen separate branches called Special Troops, which include Engineer, Chemical, Signal, Road-Building, Railroad-Building, Automotive, Construction & Billeting, Civil Defence, Rear Services, Inspectorate, Armaments and Cadres troops. These Special Troops follow the uniform dress code of the Army.

In addition to these services and support branches, the Soviet Armed forces also include two security formations, the Border Guards (GB) and the Interior Army (VV). These two forces are under the control of the Council of Ministers, the highest state ruling body for the Soviet Armed Forces, but they do not come under the control of the Ministry of Defence. The Border Guards are the KGB's military force for guarding the frontiers of the USSR. The KGB has other military units which are used to guard state officials and certain facilities such as nuclear weapon storage areas. The Interior

Army is the military wing of the MVD, the state security service responsible for internal security which also controls the regional and local police (Militia). Interior Army troops are used to guard prison camps (*gulags*), certain storehouses and government facilities, and large ammunition dumps. Most cities have a small Interior Army detachment to bolster local police in the event of trouble, and the Interior Army is also used on military bases to patrol weapon and ammunition storage areas and to prevent mutinies.

The Strategic Missile Force

The Strategic Missile Force (*Raketniye Voiska Strategicheskovo Naznacheniya:* RVSN) is considered the primary service of the Soviet Armed Forces. It was formed in 1959 as an independent service, previously having been under the control of the Artillery branch of the Ground Forces. The RVSN

is the service responsible for Soviet intermediate range and intercontinental range ballistic missiles; it means the missile silos scattered across the USSR. The major RVSN bases, and their associated missile systems, are listed on page 12.

Unlike its American counterpart, the Strategic Air Command, the RVSN does not control Soviet intercontinental strategic bombers. The RVSN has first pick of all conscripts and it would appear that it bases its recruiting policies both on high educational requirements and on security considerations. In view of the type of equipment it operates and develops, the RVSN receives the cream of the crop from secondary schools and

The Soviet Army rejuvenated its mountain infantry units in the 1980s, presumably in response to experience in Afghanistan. This new waterproof mountain uniform is easily distinguished by its dark olive colour, and the drawstrings gathering the trouser legs. The helmet net is a relatively new feature for the Soviet Army.

For some unexplained reason these Motor Rifle troops on winter exercises in March 1985 wear the new coarse burlap summer KLMK camouflage suit over their Field Dress. The helmets are worn over the *ushanka* pile cap—those of the soldier with the *Nedelya* newspaper and the man behind him are the newer SSh-60 model. Note faint red star outline painted on helmet fronts. (Sovfoto)

higher educational facilities. Its personnel appear to contain a higher percentage of Russians than any other service since it is felt that these troops are, by and large, better educated and more loyal. Although about ten per cent of RVSN troops are from the national minorities, these personnel are used in support rôles—e.g. as cooks, construction troops, etc—and not in technical or security positions. Recruits must have a clean political record. Posting to the RVSN has its advantages and its drawbacks. On the one hand, the greater technical skills warrant higher average ranks, and higher special pay—food and lodging at the RVSN facilities are a good deal better than at many other military bases. On the other hand, most RSVN bases are out in the hinterlands, with little opportunity for recreational activities off base.

RVSN Missile Bases

Yedrova	SS-17 *Spanker*
Kozielsk	SS-11 *Sego*, SS-19 *Stilleto*
Derazhnya	SS-19 *Stilleto*
Pervomaysk	SS-19 *Stilleto*
Tatishchevo	SS-19 *Stilleto*
Kostromo	SS-11 *Sego*, SS-17 *Spanker*
Teykovo	SS-11 *Sego*
Yoshkar Ola	SS-13 *Savage*
Perm	SS-11 *Sego*
Dombarovskiy	SS-18 *Satan*
Kartaly	SS-18 *Satan*
Imeni Gastello	SS-18 *Satan*
Uzhur	SS-18 *Satan*
Gladkaya	SS-11 *Sego*
Aleysk	
Drovyanaya	SS-11 *Sego*
Zhangiz Tobe	SS-18 *Satan*
Svobodniy	SS-11 *Sego*
Olovyannaya	SS-11 *Sego*
Plesetsk	Test range
Kapustin Yar	Test range
Tyuratam	Test centre

Furthermore, service in the RVSN significantly limits the chances for later obtaining visas to travel abroad.

The Ground Forces

The Ground Forces (*Sukhoputniye Voiska*) are the largest single service in the Soviet Armed Forces. In Europe or America this service would be called the Army. The Ground forces have five principal branches; the Motor Rifle Troops, Tank Troops, Rocket and Artillery Troops, Army Air Defence Troops and Army Aviation Troops. About 70 per cent of all Soviet conscripts end up in the Ground Forces. The Ground Forces do not rank particularly high in priority as far as recruitment is concerned. The more technically-oriented services such as the RVSN, Air Forces, PVO and navy tend to draw away many of the better educated recruits, and the security requirements of the other services tend to drain away a disproportionate percentage of the more reliable Slavic national groups. The Soviet Army, like the Tsarist Army before it, would prefer to draw more heavily on Russian conscripts for its combat and technical units. This is due to the language problem, particularly in the non-slavic minority groups, and also, as mentioned earlier, to Russian perceptions of the loyalty of other ethnic groups. Inevitably, the Ground Forces receive a significant number of recruits from the minorities, particularly from Central Asia: non-Slavic troops probably constitute about 30 per cent of the recruits in the Ground Forces. Soviet policy has been to ensure that these troops do not constitute a majority in any combat unit of significant size (probably battalion level). Since they will inevitably receive recruits from the national minorities, the Ground Forces attempt to select troops from towns and cities where there is a greater chance that the recruit will have picked up some Russian in school. There is no remedial language training in the Soviet Armed Forces; if you don't speak Russian when you enter the service, you will learn it the hard way, or else . . .

The combat organisation of the Ground Forces is primarily built around two basic types of divisions;

Motor Rifle squad dismounted in defensive position, the foreground soldier with an RPG-7. Regulations forbid the use of the red/yellow Everyday Dress insignia on the greatcoat for field exercises, but they are very often seen, largely because each soldier has only one coat to wear for several orders of dress. The small gold-on-red embroidered stripes worn on each arm by the two nearest men indicate that they have served for one year in the Ground Forces. (Sovfoto)

the motor rifle division and the tank division. In 1986 there were a total of 142 motor rifle divisions and 51 tank divisions, according to US sources. However, it should be noted that not all Soviet units are kept at full strength during peacetime. NATO intelligence generally categorises Soviet Ground Forces divisions as Category 1, Category 2, and Category 3. A Category 1 division is at a wartime readiness level, with 75 to 110 per cent of its troops and equipment at hand. A Category 2 division is deployable in about 10–30 days and has 50–75 per cent of its troops at hand, and about 90 per cent of its equipment. A Category 3, or cadre division, is deployable in about 60 days by fleshing it out with reservists, and has only 10–35 per cent of its troops and 35–50 per cent of its equipment at hand. Category 1 divisions usually have the prime equipment (such as T-64, T-72 or T-80 tanks), while Category 2 divisions have older equipment

(like T-62 or T-55 tanks), and Category 3 divisions scrape the bottom of the barrel for equipment and troops. About a third of all divisions are at each of these levels. The different categories of divisions are not evenly divided: divisions in Central Europe with the Groups of Forces are uniformly Category 1, as are most divisions in the western Soviet military districts. Divisions in the interior of the USSR are usually of the poorest quality, while units facing China are about 15 per cent Category 1 and 35 per cent Category 2.

The Airborne Assault Force

The Airborne Assault Force (*Vozdushno-Desantnaya Voyska*: VDV) is a semi-autonomous element of the Soviet Army, with traditional links to both the Air Forces and the Ground Forces. The VDV is the primary strategic reserve force of the Soviet high command, and could be expected to receive particularly challenging tasks in the event of war. The VDV numbers seven divisions, and has played a particularly prominent rôle in Soviet actions outside the USSR since 1945, such as the seizure of

Lt. S. Sukhenkiy directs the fire of one of his platoon's PKM machine guns during winter exercises in Siberia, February 1977. He wears subdued olive collar tabs, while his men wear the red tabs of Motor Rifle troops. (Sovfoto)

A senior lieutenant (left) and a major of a Motor Rifle regiment confer during exercises in March 1981. Both wear the *obchina* sheepskin greatcoat authorised for arctic regions. The lieutenant carries a red and white signal flag, to call forward his unit under conditions of radio silence. (Sovfoto)

Prague in the 1968 Czechoslovakia invasion, and the 1979 invasion of Afghanistan. For this reason the VDV enjoys preferential treatment in the selection of recruits. While the VDV does not have the priority afforded the Strategic Missile Forces, there is only limited friction between the recruiting requirements of these services, since they are each looking for a different type of recruit: the VDV places more stress on athletic skills compared to the Strategic Missile Force's search for recruits with higher academic skills. The VDV's main recruiting grounds are the parachute clubs of DOSAAF.

The Air Forces

The Air Forces (*Voyenno-Vozdushniye Sily*: VVS) are the third most senior service of the Soviet Armed Forces. The VVS has three main forces: Frontal Aviation (FA), Long-Range Aviation (DA) and Transport Aviation (VTA)—these roughly correspond to SAC, TAC and MAC in the US Air Force. Frontal Aviation is the largest force, and contains all tactical combat aircraft such as fighters, ground attack aircraft and military helicopters. The Long-Range Aviation is the strategic nuclear attack force, and is equipped with intercontinental bombers, as well as supporting aircraft such as aerial tankers. The Transport Aviation branch includes all large, fixed-wing transport aircraft.

The Air Forces require a technically talented pool of recruits, and are allotted a level of priority somewhat less than the Strategic Missile Force, but considerably more than the Ground Forces. The Air Forces can pre-select some recruits for specialised positions, especially pilots, from the aspiring ranks of young trainees in the DOSAAF sailplane and aviation clubs. These clubs can also serve as a recruitment ground for other specialised skills, such as mechanics. As in the case of the Strategic Missile Force, the Air Forces prefer, and tend to receive, a larger percentage of Slavic recruits. Not surprisingly, service in the Air Forces is popular, and the life of military pilots is glamorised in the Soviet press. The service tour for many specialists in the Air Force is longer than for conscripts into the Ground Forces, but the pay is better, living conditions more comfortable and the food more palatable.

The Air Defence Forces

The Air Defence Forces (*Protivozdushnaya Oborona Voysk*: PVO) were formed in 1947 by breaking off the air defence artillery units from the Ground Forces. The PVO has been the subject of continuing changes since 1981, heavily affecting its basic organisation. There are currently four or five major branches of the PVO. Interceptor Aviation (IA-PVO) controls air defence interceptor regiments, equipped with aircraft like the MiG-25 and Su-15. This element of the PVO has been the most heavily affected by recent changes: while IA-PVO had controlled all interceptors, since the changes in the early 1980s it now only controls interceptor units in the interior military districts. Interceptors in the border regions were turned over to the Frontal Aviation branch of the Air Forces. The largest element of the PVO is the Zenith Missile Forces (ZRV) which control anti-aircraft missile forces. The ZRV is primarily responsible for fixed air defence sites in the USSR and abroad, using such systems as the S-75 (SA-2 *Guideline*), S-125 (SA-3 *Goa*) and S-200 (SA-5 *Gammon*). The ZRV is also administratively responsible for the mobile air defence missile units by the Ground Forces, such as the units equipped with the ZRK Kub (SA-6

An artillery command post during February 1975 exercises in the Siberian Military District. Sheepskin coats are not common among enlisted men, but are seen in areas where winter is especially severe. The cap badges identify the second man from left as an officer, the others as privates or NCOs. (Sovfoto)

Gainful), ZRK Strela 1 (SA-9 *Gaskin*), ZRK Krug (SA-4 *Ganef*), etc. The ZRV operates the schools at which the Ground Forces air defence officers are trained, and apparently administers the design and development of the Ground Forces air defence weapons. However, these mobile air defence units are under Ground Forces tactical control.

The Radio-Technical Force (RTV) branch encompasses the radar and other electronic sites associated with the PVO. This branch controls the radar sites used to survey the Soviet frontier, and trains the troops who man the radars associated with the ZRV's air defence missile regiments.

The most enigmatic elements of the PVO are the Space Defence (PKO) and Anti-missile Defence (PRO) branches. The Anti-missile Defence branch mans and operates the anti-ballistic missile sites around Moscow, equipped with the UR-96 (ABM-1 *Galosh*) and ABM-3 *Gazelle* missile systems. The

PKO is responsible for space defence, which would presumably include anti-missile (ASAT) efforts as well as the Soviet equivalent of the US Strategic Defence Initiative (SDI, 'Star Wars') programme. Little is known of either branch.

The PVO shares a similar recruiting priority level with the Air Forces.

The Special Troops

Special Troops is the term applied to the non-combat support elements of the Soviet Army. Some of these, such as the Engineer Troops and Chemical Defence Troops, are highly trained, combat-capable units comparable to the normal Ground Forces units with which they serve. These services are not unlike the Ground Forces in terms of recruiting practices.

The majority of the Special Troops, sometimes called Rear Forces (such as the Road Troops, Railroad Troops and Construction & Billeting Troops), receive little or no combat training and have no immediate counterparts in most NATO armies. These support troops serve in functions that would be performed by civil engineering and construction firms in most NATO countries; however, in the Soviet Union there has long been a tradition of Army involvement in large construction projects (for example, Special Troops played a prominent rôle in the construction of the new Baikal-Amur Magistral rail line in the Far East in recent years).

Furthermore, the support services provide a niche in which conscripts unwanted by the combat arms can serve their two years of military service. The groups singled out for these rôles are the least assimilated or most suspect of the national minorities, or conscripts who have criminal or political records. About half of the Construction Troops are Central Asians, especially those from rural backgrounds who have little or no knowledge of Russian; and another 20 per cent are from the Caucasus' such as Armenians and Georgians. They are assigned to menial tasks, and training is negligible. Other minorities, such as Jews, West Ukrainians and Balts, are disproportionately represented in the support services; however, since they are apt to be from urban backgrounds, understand Russian and are relatively well educated, they quickly find their way into the NCO ranks or into other responsible posts. An officer in one of these *stroibat* (construction battalions) described the typical breakdown of labour in such a unit: Russians would operate any specialised equipment such as construction machinery; Ukrainians, Jews and other Europeans would be used to lay cable in the building under construction; and the remaining troops would be used to dig ditches or perform any other physical tasks.

Welcome to the Army, Ivan Ivanovich!

Conscript levies take place twice a year in the Soviet Union, in April–May and after the harvest in October–November. Each year about 75 per cent of all eligible 18-year-old men are drafted; the remainder receive deferments. There are three principal types of deferment, on educational, health or hardship grounds. Educational deferments apply

Soldiers of the Caucasian Military District receive offerings of food from local citizens in native folk dress during the Kavkaz-85 exercises designed to simulate combat between the USSR and southern NATO forces in Turkey. The exercise saw the introduction of this new camouflaged helmet cover.

The crew of a BMP-1 of the Rezhitskaya Guards Motor Rifle Division ('Panfilov') in September 1981. Cpl. Rustam Tursunov (left) is the driver; he and the gunner, Pte. Alimbek Nasilov (right) wear black tanker's coveralls. The commander, Sr.Sgt. Ivan Bochorskiy (centre), wears normal Motor Rifles uniform in Field configuration. Note signal flags in canvas belt-holster. He would replace his tanker's helmet with a steel helmet when leaving the vehicle to lead the dismounted squad in combat.

to young men accepted into certain institutes of higher learning, including universities and certain vocational training schools. These men will later be eligible for the annual draft, unless they join an officers' training programme at their school. Health deferments apply both to young men with permanent disabilities and to those with temporary medical problems which make service in a given year impossible; those with temporary problems will be drafted later. Hardship deferments include men who are the sole support of elderly parents who cannot support themselves, fathers of at least two children, and similar cases. Although some young men in each age-bracket escape the first troop-levy, most are eventually brought under the colours. Only about 12 per cent of Soviet young men manage to escape military service altogether.

The new conscripts report to the local *voenkomat* (Military Commissariat) in their city or district for induction. Recruitment practices vary considerably. A central element in this procedure is the *pokupatel*, literally, a 'military buyer'. Several

pokupatels will visit a particular Military Commissariat with papers entitling them to a given number of recruits; the papers outline the number of troops, qualifications and ethnic backgrounds desired. The *pokupatels* represent either entire military districts or individual units.

On the basis of documents collected since the recruit first registered at the Military Commissariat at the age of 17, some pre-selection of recruits is done for special training. Recruits who show special aptitude or leadership ability are singled out for NCO school. The Soviet Army does not rely on a professional NCO class as do most NATO armies. Indeed, only about 5 per cent of all NCOs are professionals, the remainder being conscripts. NCOs are recruited from the annual draftees, and serve a two-year term like the rest of the men from their age group. Many of the NCO candidates are selected at induction, but a portion are selected later on the basis of their performance during initial training. Special pre-selection is also made of candidates for officer school, aircrew training, the VDV airborne force and other élite postings.

A common technique used by the *pokupatels* to 'buy' their troops is simply to load a given number of conscripts on to a train destined for a particular military district. During the course of the trip, the *pokupatels* will 'buy' the troops they need for their unit or military district, and each recruit will be informed of the results. These train trips can be quite lengthy, since the Soviet Army has a policy of stationing troops away from their homes. In the case of many of the minority nationalities, there is a policy to station them completely outside their national republics.

The initial experiences of a Soviet conscript soldier vary. In some cases, the conscript is sent directly to his unit to undergo training. In other cases, he will report to a special unit at the military district for training, after which he will be transferred to his unit. Basic training for the ranks is four weeks for most—shorter than in most NATO armies, since there is the presumption that pre-induction training in school has already covered many matters. During the four week 'quarantined' training period, the conscript is issued his uniforms and equipment, receives medical treatment (mostly consisting of inoculations and examinations), and is given a rough-and-tumble basic military training.

For about a third of the conscripts, life is somewhat different. These conscripts, selected at induction for NCO or specialist training, are sent to NCO or specialist schools, often located in special training divisions. These future NCOs receive the same four-week quarantined period for basic training and induction, followed by five months of specialist training.

The Annual Training Cycle

In the Soviet Union military life follows a seasonal pattern tied to the bi-annual induction of draftees. At any one time a quarter of the troops in tank and motor rifle divisions are new recruits and, likewise, twice a year a quarter of the army returns to civilian life in a mass exodus unmatched in most other European countries.

In October, while the inductees are in transit from their homes, the summer training period comes to a close, and about a quarter of the troops prepare to leave military service. At this time the first batch of new junior officers arrive, fresh from the military academies, or from civilian universities where they were enlisted on officer training courses. In November the new crop of NCOs, inducted in the previous April–May draft, have completed their training in training divisions and arrive at their division in time to greet the new inductees. At this time the conscripts also undergo their four weeks of basic training. November marks the end of one training year, and December the beginning of the next. The Minister of Defence makes a major speech which outlines the special focus of the new year's training. In December the first unit training begins as part of the winter training schedule. Unit training will begin at platoon level, and work its way through company and battalion levels.

The winter training period ends in May. As in the previous November, that quarter of the troops who have completed their two-year active duty obligation are released into the reserves. The NCOs who had been inducted in October–November have completed their six-month training and arrive at their divisions along with the new conscripts. The four-week basic training is completed in May, and in June the summer training period begins.

Jr.Sgt. Mikhail Vangela and Pte. Pavel Silnechko, crewmen of a T-55A(M) tank during exercises in the Transcarpathian Military District in August 1978. They wear typical black tanker's coveralls with four pockets, and the yellow tank insignia on the right breast. The black beret is worn by most Armoured Force crews in place of the *pilotka*. (Sovfoto)

Capts. A. Artyshenko and N. Kovalev confer on their T-55K command tank during exercises in the Siberian Military District, November 1975. Both wear subdued shoulder boards, whose olive colour contrasts with the black coveralls.

Garrison Life

The daily life of a Soviet conscript is heavily regimented, monotonous and sometimes brutal. Very little free time is allowed to new recruits, on the assumption that they will only get into some form of mischief. Idle time is filled with repetitive drills, or 'make-work' projects: there are always some rocks desperately in need of a coat of whitewash, or some trench which needs digging— or filling—or both . . . The style of life in Soviet barracks is more traditional than is now the case in most NATO countries, and would not be unfamiliar to a European or American soldier of the last century.

Life in the barracks is stratified by seniority and ethnicity, and at the top of the heap are the senior sergeants. Usually, after two years of service, most conscripts will have risen to NCO rank; these

sergeants wear a two-year duty stripe. Below them are soldiers from later drafts, with a year-and-a-half's seniority, a year's seniority, or six-months' seniority. At the bottom of the heap are the new recruits, who do the filthiest jobs, and are subjected to a certain amount of harassment by senior troops.

Non-Russian troops are also subjected to a degree of harassment. Less favoured minorities, especially the Central Asians, suffer a certain amount of verbal and physical abuse. Ethnic slurs, such as *chuchmyek* or *churka*, are virtually universal, to say nothing of the more salty expressions. Barracks break up into ethnic cliques: Ukrainians with Ukrainians, Uzbeks with Uzbeks, etc. These groups form to protect one another, to speak a common tongue, and to commiserate with one another over their fate. The Soviet Army does not offer any Russian language training programme after induction, and so these cliques can help to ease the adjustment of new recruits who speak only a little Russian or none at all. The Soviet Army has suffered from a fair amount of ethnic tension and brawling in the past decade, but some Soviet emigrés say that this is not viewed as so much of a problem as, e.g. the racial tensions in the US Army in the 1970s. Indeed, some ex-Soviet servicemen say that the ethnic tensions are sometimes encouraged by officers who feel that such tensions make it easier to control the units, since hostility is vented towards other soldiers rather than towards the commanders.

Conditions in the garrison are spartan by Western standards. Sanitary conditions in many garrisons are basic, and in the field they are worse; diseases such as hepatitis and dysentery are not uncommon in some areas, and have been very serious under field conditions, e.g. in Afghanistan. Army food is bland, and often insufficient, and Soviet emigrés who served in the Ground Forces remember hunger as a universal feature of army life. But to draftees from the Soviet hinterlands these conditions are not as unfamiliar or as harsh as they might seem to a Western European or American. Most young Soviet recruits, especially Russians and Ukrainians, are patriotic in an old-fashioned way, and regard their tour of duty as a normal obligation which must be endured. The patriotic sentiment is not necessarily shared by the ethnic minorities, but the Army can offer some opportunities to recruits from the USSR's forgotten backwaters.

The Daily Schedule

Reveille is at 6.00 am, followed by about 40 minutes to clean up, make up the bunk and do calisthenics. At 6.50 am, there is an inspection, or a lecture by the unit's political officer (*zampolit*) on 'world political highlights'. Political indoctrination is a major concern of the Soviet leadership, and is the bane of the Soviet citizen's existence, whether soldier or civilian. At 7.25 am, the unit goes off to the mess for breakfast.

Usually breakfast is served family style, with each squad occupying a single table in the mess hall. NCOs and more senior soldiers from previous levies often take advantage of the newer recruits by taking larger portions of food. In the Soviet Army, as in Soviet society, benefits flow from rank and seniority. The normal breakfast, which amounts to about a quarter of the food issued daily to troops, consists of two slices of white bread, a slice of black bread, 20 grammes (less than an ounce) of butter or margarine, 300 grammes (about 10 oz, or .65 lbs) of either *kasha* (a grain porridge) or potatoes, and 50 grammes (1.7 oz) of meat or fish. Meat, infrequently served, is often the unforgettable 'head cheese', which is a sausage made from some of the less desirable extremities of some hapless creature. Fish is more common, and is normally *selyodka*, a common type of Russian salted herring. This hearty if bland meal is washed down by several helpings of the ever popular *chai* (tea), sweetened with up to three cubes of sugar per breakfast issue.

Officers are fed separately, cafeteria style, and

Maj. I. P. Kolosov teaches officer candidates at the Blagoveshchensk Higher Tank Command School in the Far East Military District, May 1975. The soldiers are still wearing the black padded winter jacket and coveralls issued to tank troops. (Sovfoto)

Maj. V. Savenkov, commander of an R-17E (SS-1c '*Scud*') rocket battalion on exercises in October 1982, gives instructions to two of his launcher commanders, a lieutenant and a senior lieutenant. Crews of specialised vehicles like the MAZ-543P launch vehicle for the R-17 wear black tank coveralls and other items of tankers' uniform. The major wears the usual subdued Field Dress version of the officers' peaked cap. (Sovfoto)

receive a better selection of food including dairy products, eggs and fruit. It is an invariable rule in the Soviet Army that the conscripts receive the poorest grade of food, the NCOs a somewhat better selection (if only due to their own efforts in 'accepting' offerings from the conscripts) and the officers the best, though still depending somewhat on rank.

Daily Training

Daily training begins at 8.00 am and lasts about six hours. The details vary from branch to branch; as the most common types of units are the motor rifle regiments and tank regiments, these merit a more detailed examination.

Soviet training contains many of the elements common to all military training, stressing physical fitness, hardiness and unquestioning obedience to the instructions of superior officers. The Soviets have been heavily influenced by their experiences in the Second World War, when shortages of even the most basic supplies were endemic, and soldiers often had to forage for food. While peacetime conditions are not as severe as this, Soviet training practices do not encourage reliance on extensive logistical support for their combat arm. Ammunition and fuel take priority, if necessary to the exclusion of all else.

This affects many areas which NATO troops would take for granted. Field sleeping practices are a good example. In nearly all northern NATO armies troops are issued with a sleeping bag for cold weather field conditions. When questioned about the seeming lack of sleeping bags in the Soviet Ground Forces, a number of emigré Soviet ex-servicemen expressed astonishment that anyone would even expect Soviet infantrymen to receive such luxuries. According to them, the usual practice is to send a foraging party into the woods to cut down boughs; in the steppes they substitute sheaves of oats, hay or other suitable material. These are laid on the ground or placed in a shallow entrenchment to form a primitive mattress, on which the soldier sleeps in his greatcoat. The only sleeping bags that these soldiers had ever seen were rare examples purchased privately by officers from sporting goods stores.

The same applies to load-carrying equipment. Soviet troops are not regularly issued with rucksacks except for certain specialised rôles (such as the rocket grenade rucksacks for RPG-7 teams). Although military rucksacks do exist in both small and large sizes, they are relatively uncommon, and appear to be reserved for specialised units such as mountain or airborne troops. What personal gear the troops need is carried in the armoured personnel carrier. (It should be kept in mind that the emigré accounts on which these statements are based refer to the Soviet Army of nearly ten years ago, and things may have changed; however, there is little or no evidence of such changes in the Soviet military press.)

The emphasis on hardiness is sometimes carried to extremes. It is very uncommon to see Soviet troops wearing eyeglasses. This is to some extent due to the notion that young men *should not* need eyeglasses—and therefore are not issued them.

Infantry Training

Weapons training is not dissimilar to that carried out in most armies. The Soviet Army does not, however, appear to provide as much live small arms practice and basic rifle drill as most NATO armies, and appears still to place greater emphasis on basic drill and parade practice. Part of the reason behind the less extensive live firing is the expense; part is also due to Soviet infantry tradition since the Second World War, which stresses massed fire, not precision marksmanship. The reliance of the Red Army of the Second World War on the PPSh sub-machine gun has carried over to the AK family of assault rifles. Soviet infantrymen are trained in aimed fire, but field exercises also stress firing from the hip while charging forward in conjunction with armoured troop carriers. It is felt that in the heat of battle, aimed fire from infantrymen is too much to

Medics bring a 'casualty' back to a LuAZ-969 ambulance jeep during 1981 exercises in Czechoslovakia. The 'casualty' wears the ShMS gas mask with voice device; the man on his right, the OP-1 CBR suit and standard ShM mask: cf.Plate L.

Medics 'under fire', pulling the driver out of a BMP with a special crew evacuation harness. Note red cross armbands, and the fact that all the medics are armed with AK-74 rifles.

be expected. What precision marksmanship is required can be provided by snipers, who are available in larger numbers in the Soviet Army than in NATO armies.

The basic tactical unit of the motor rifle formations is the squad or section (*otdyeleniye*). The infantry squad has varied in size and composition since the 1960s, but has gradually stabilised at a dismountable squad of seven to nine men, depending upon the type of mechanised vehicle in the unit. This total does not include the other two squad members, the vehicle driver and vehicle gunner, who generally remain in the BTR or BMP during combat. The exact composition of a squad depends on its position in the company. In a normal motor rifle platoon (*vzvod*) with three squads, the first a nine-man dismountable squad consists of the platoon leader (a lieutenant), the squad leader (a sergeant), two squad machine gunners (with PKMs), four riflemen (with AKMs or AK-74s), an additional rifleman with an SVD sniper rifle and an anti-tank grenadier with an RPG-7 or RPG-16. The second squad is usually smaller with eight dismountable men including a squad leader, one or two squad machine gunners, an anti-tank grenadier, and four or five riflemen. The third squad is configured like the first, but has the platoon sergeant in lieu of the platoon lieutenant, and a

Strela 2 air defence missile operator (SA-7 *Grail* or SA-14 *Gremlin*) in place of the sniper.

The platoon leader (lieutenant) is normally authorised a pistol, but these days may carry an AKSU carbine. The squad leaders are all sergeants, and carry an AKM or AK-74 rifle and 120 rounds of ammunition (a 30-round clip in the rifle, three magazines in the ammunition pouch). These squad leaders are normally conscript sergeants, often straight out of their initial six-month training course. They are the best-trained men in the squad, and the only ones (apart from the platoon lieutenant and platoon sergeant) who are trained in map reading and basic radio communications. The squad leaders are also usually cross-trained as BTR or BMP drivers and gunners.

The two PKM squad machine guns are allotted 1,000 rounds each, and this is spread out among the squad. Some units use the RPK-74, older RPK or other automatic weapons rather than the PKM. Usually two of the squad riflemen are assigned as assistant machine gunners for the PKMs. Although details are lacking, it would appear that some units are receiving the AGS-17 automatic grenade launcher in place of at least one PKM. This would probably require the attention of two squad members to carry the weapon, the tripod and associated ammunition. The RPG-7 grenadier can be allotted either a pistol or an AK, the latter apparently being more common. Usually one squad rifleman is the RPG assistant, and carries a special rucksack with four additional rocket grenade rounds. Each platoon has a sniper with an SVD rifle. Such widespread distribution of sniper rifles is traditional in the Russian Army, and is also rooted in the mass fire tradition explained above, which places less stress on marksmanship for the average infantryman compared, for example, with the US Army.

The most sophisticated weapon in the motor rifle platoon is the *Strela 2* (9M32M) air defence missile, better known in NATO as the SA-7 *Grail* (currently being replaced by the SA-14 *Gremlin*). The *Strela 2* is a small, man-portable launcher firing an infra-red guided missile. The newer SA-14 *Gremlin* appears to be a laser-beam-riding guided missile. These missiles provide the platoon with a degree of air defence against low-flying aircraft and helicopters. The missile comes in a disposable launch tube; once fired, the tube is discarded, and a new round mounted on the basic gripstock assembly. It would appear that most platoons carry two rounds of missile ammunition.

The two vehicle crewmen attached to the squad, the mechanic/driver and gunner, are both considered specialists and so are usually sergeants. The driver is normally armed with a pistol and the gunner with an AK, but since the advent of the AKSU carbine both may use this weapon.

Special weapons training in the Soviet Ground Forces tends to place heavier reliance on simulators than on live fire. This is particularly true of expensive weapons like the SA-7 *Grail*. Even small arms training sometimes features air rifles for marksmanship practice.

Squad and platoon tactical training tends to be more formalised than in many NATO armies, placing great stress on battle drills and standardised dismounting and attack formations. While this is sometimes cited as evidence of the Soviet tendency to stifle individual initiative, the Soviets feel that battle drills, repeatedly practised and memorised by rote, are more suitable in real combat conditions for the average Soviet infantryman. They contend that under normal combat conditions—with the soldiers exhausted, frightened, or both—the basic drills will be followed automatically, allowing the squad, platoon and company leaders to employ their troops to best effect. Soviet tactical training has not yet included widespread employment of the revolutionary laser training devices entering service in NATO, and indeed, much of the field training has remained unchanged since the 1960s.

In comparison to NATO mechanised infantry squads, Soviet squads are poorly trained and led. The responsibility for training and leadership falls on a non-professional sergeant who has had only five months of training when he takes up his duties. The common NATO practice is to break up squads into fire teams, with their own leaders to assist the squad sergeant; but the Soviet squad leader's assistant is the vehicle gunner, who is too remote to assist in the control of dismounted action. Soviet platoons have only a single dismountable radio, usually carried with the platoon leader; this means that the squad leader has no radio contact with his vehicle, or with other elements of the platoon unless they are in sight and can be signalled visually. To

Soviet Air Force officer candidates display the VVS's uniform, essentially similar to that of the Ground Forces but with pale blue collar tabs and shoulder boards and the VVS arm patch backed in pale blue. The four embroidered gold stripes indicate that this student has been four years at this military school; they have alternate coloured backgrounds—red for odd years (one, three and five) and pale blue, as here, for even years (two, four).

call for fire support from his vehicle the squad leader can only point or fire tracer at the target.

Tank Training

Soviet tankers require more specialised training than infantrymen, so not surprisingly, most crewmen in a tank may be sergeants. The crews of Soviet tanks consist of four men in the older T-54, T-55 and T-62 tanks, and three men in the newer T-64, T-72 and T-80. The difference in crew size is because the loader can be dispensed with on the newer tanks, which are fitted with an auto-loading system. Generally, on the older tanks, the loader is the only non-specialist in the crew, and the only member who is unlikely to be a sergeant. The three remaining crewmen are the driver/mechanic, gunner and vehicle commander, who receive six months of specialised training on induction.

Basic crew weapons training in the Soviet Union places heavier emphasis on simulators than on actual use of the equipment. Tanks are usually limited to about 250 km of travel annually, which is not really sufficient to train and keep the drivers proficient. Soviet tanks tend to use more primitive clutch and brake steering than NATO tanks, and so are more difficult to operate. As a result, driver simulators are used for additional practice. Acquisition of gunnery skills is also somewhat hampered by meagre allotments of training ammunition; Soviet tank crews fire only about a dozen rounds of live main gun ammunition annually, compared to up to ten times that much in the US Army. As a substitute 23mm sub-calibre devices are fitted into the tubes for firing simulation; this is perfectly adequate for certain gunnery skills, but fails to build up practice in crew interaction such as rapid target acquisition, loading, firing, retargeting, reloading, etc.

As in the infantry, considerable stress is placed on battle drills and standardised formations in tactical training. Most Soviet tank units have small training grounds with a variety of targets for gunnery practice and tactical exercise. One of the main inhibitions to tactical exercises above squad or platoon strength is the limitation placed on the

number of hours a tank can be operated annually. It is not uncommon for tank regiments to have only a single platoon of tanks operational in each of its three battalions for training purposes, with the rest in temporary storage. These are taken out for periodic battalion- and regimental-scale exercises, which include both tactical and gunnery drills to demonstrate the proficiency of the crews.

Tactical tank training has been the subject of a fair amount of criticism in the Soviet military press. Most of these exercises are scored, and apparently it is an all too common practice to lay out tactical exercises in a very regular and regimented fashion to ensure high scores: low scores would give a poor impression to senior officers, and would do little to improve career chances for the unit commanders. In general, Soviet training doctrine pays a great deal of lip service to creativity and initiative on the part of tank officers, but the actual organisational features of the training cycle serve to discourage these principles. Soviet tank training is qualitatively and quantitatively inferior to average NATO training, but it is not clear whether these shortcomings are sufficient to undermine the Soviet

Officers outside one of the oldest and most prestigious military academies, the M. V. Frunze Military Academy in Moscow. They wear Everyday Dress with greatcoats.

Ground Forces' numerical advantages over NATO tank units.

Back to the Mess Hall

Following the daily training, the main meal of the day is served around 2.00 pm. It begins with soup or *borshch*. The main course is *kasha*, but unlike the morning serving this is usually livened up with onions and seasoning and a few pieces of meat. Normally it is served with a slice of white bread and two slices of black bread, but without margarine or butter. Finally, some form of cooked fruit is served, either *kissel* (stewed fruit in a thickened jelly) or *kompot*, (boiled fruit in a sweet, watery juice). *Kompot* is usually the only beverage served at lunch. Lunch lasts about 40 minutes, and the troops are then given a half-hour rest period and a further 20 minutes to take care of their personal equipment.

At 3.30 pm the next training session begins: on Mondays and Thursdays the omnipresent and numbingly soporific political education courses; on Tuesdays and Fridays, equipment maintenance. Wednesdays and Saturday afternoons are devoted to organised sports, usually the ever popular *futbol*. The troops are then given about an hour for personal study until 7.40 pm. This is usually devoted to mastering specialist skills and preparing for the associated exam. Enthusiasm for the specialist skills qualification is due to the fact that in the Soviet Army men who do not qualify for specialists skills do not receive any home leave for the two years of service. The specialist qualifications are rated at 3rd Class, 2nd Class, 1st Class and Master, and there are pay bonuses for each of these grades as well. The qualification badges associated with passing these tests are regularly worn on the service uniform, on the right breast. The pay bonuses are particularly important, since conscripts' pay is miserly: privates receive about 4.30 rubles monthly (about £4 sterling or $7.50 US), and a conscript junior sergeant receives about 11.80 rubles. This money is quickly spent on food at the division snack shop or on cigarettes if not supplemented by specialist pay. Specialist pay covers such rôles as tank drivers or gunners, missile crewmen, chemical defence specialists, and communication operators. Certain soldiers are excluded, including basic riflemen or tank loaders.

Supper lasts half an hour, until 8.10 pm, and is similar to breakfast, but usually fish is served. The evening fish ration is supposed to be 100 grammes (3.5 oz) each, and can be boiled, fried or marinated, but is usually salted herring. Besides the fish, there are 300 grammes of potatoes or *kasha*, a couple of slices of white bread and a slice of black bread, 20 grammes of butter, and tea.

The quality of the food in a unit is largely dependent on the division's officers and the regimental ration supply officers. The basic food allotments to Soviet divisions are very skimpy. Canned goods come from the food industry and perishable goods from local farms, or the *voyenniy sovkhoz*—military farms in each military district. Even this is barely adequate. Many regiments have their own 'kitchen farms' which raise pigs, rabbits and chickens to supplement the meat rations. The pigs are kept to take care of kitchen refuse, and are saved for meals on important holidays. Most regiments also raise vegetables, often in special greenhouses. This small-scale farming operation is managed by the regimental supply chief and the personnel are recruited from the troops. The current goal in the Ground Forces is to have each regiment self-sufficient enough to provide each

Lt. M. Ozhimkov prepares an artillery firing position in the Siberian Military District, September 1977. His uniform is fairly typical of officers' summer Field Dress; he wears Field shoulder boards, the rank stars in dull zinc rather than polished brass; and on his chest can be seen a Komsomol pin, a Guards badge, and two other decorations. (Sovfoto)

A senior lieutenant supervises the range finder at an artillery firing post; all wear fairly typical cold weather uniforms, the black collar tabs of the Artillery and Rocket Force standing out against the grey greatcoats. (Sovfoto)

member of the unit with 15 kg of meat annually: this translates roughly into 100 pigs and 28,000 chickens per regimental farm. About five per cent of regimental personnel are allotted to food-related work.

Another food source is local collective farms. Some unit commanders trade troop labour (on Sundays) in exchange for food from the farm. While food for the conscripts is seldom better than adequate, without some extra attention from regimental officers the food situation can cause health problems. In some units soldiers suffer from vitamin and mineral deficiencies due to lack of dietary variety, especially lack of fresh vegetables: in some cases even potatoes and cabbage may run out before a new harvest. This had led not to higher levels of supplies from the military districts, but to greater attention being given to 'kitchen farms' and similar local efforts.

The food quality is also dependent on the branch of service. Food rations are categorised on a scale running from one to four. The construction units receive the lowest (category one—2,800 cal.); tankers and motor riflemen a little more (category two—3,400 cal.); and pilots receive the highest (category four—5,000 cal.).

In spite of the legendary rôle of vodka in Russian society and culture, alcohol is strictly forbidden to enlisted men: indeed, it is a state crime to serve liquor to any serviceman in uniform, and the penalties can be severe. Nevertheless, many troops have already begun drinking before entering the service, and heavy drinking is closely associated with manliness in Russian culture. Inevitably, many soldiers attempt to get hold of alcohol in one manner or another. This sometimes leads to extreme behaviour like stealing military methanol (which can lead to severe poisoning), or drinking certain alcohol-based products like cheap perfumes. The more common remedy is *samogon*, the Russian equivalent of 'moonshine'. It is virtually impossible to set up a still in the barracks; the potatoes or grain needed for the basic raw material are too scarce, and would be eaten rather than used to make vodka. Nor would the materials or a safe hiding place for a still be easy to find. However, many farmers make their own *samogon*, and manage to turn a tidy profit by selling it to soldiers just outside their garrison gates. *Samogon* is usually cheaper than store-bought vodka. A good vodka can cost as much as seven rubles if sold to soldiers, while *samogon* is usually about three rubles per litre bottle. Alcoholism in the service is, in fact, more commonly a problem among the officers, who have readier access to liquor.

Discipline

The Soviet Army is very conscious of strict discipline. In reply to a question from an officer, a simple 'yes' (*da*) or 'no' (*nyet*) is unacceptable. The proper response is *tak tochno* (exactly so) or *nikak nyet* (not at all). The type and amount of punishment that can be imposed on a recruit depends on rank. A sergeant who commands a squad can rebuke his troops, and can give them up to seven days of garrison restrictions and up to one day of extra duty, but he cannot order confinement. A junior lieutenant, commanding a platoon, can impose up to 21 days of restriction and four days of extra duty. Only a company commander (usually a captain) can order confinement in the guardhouse for up to three days. Reduction in rank or revocation of an award, such as a specialist qualification, can come only from a regimental commander or above, meaning usually a colonel or higher.

Attitudes towards punishment vary depending upon the source. Although the Soviet Army is more discipline-conscious than many other armies, many line officers do not like to inflict punishments that will be noted officially in the records, such as guardhouse duty. They feel, rightly, that this will be regarded by higher authorities as indicative of poor leadership in the unit. The preferred method of imposing discipline within units is by unrecorded punishment. One of the most frequent forms of punishment is deprival of leave. Soviet recruits normally get two days' leave a month, which is usually spent in neighbouring towns. In view of the dreariness of life on base, leaves are precious, and the threat of deprival is often sufficient to convince a recalcitrant recruit to shape up. If this doesn't work, officers can get one of the unit's sergeants to pound the stuffing out of the recruit (unofficially, of course . . .).

The other arms of authority take a different view on punishments. Military police of the Commandant's Service are often given quotas to fill when patrolling towns or the like, and so guardhouse time is awarded rather liberally.

Maj.Gen. M. M. Zaitsev at his divisional command post during the Dniepr exercises of 1970. Note that no rank insignia are displayed on the KLMK camouflage coveralls, even when worn by general officers.

Leadership

The Soviet NCO

As mentioned above, the vast majority of sergeants and other NCOs in the army are regular two-year conscripts who receive an initial six-month specialist training at the beginning of their career. The Soviet NCO fills a somewhat different rôle than his counterpart in Western armies, where there is the tradition of a professional NCO class. NCOs fill many postings that would be occupied by lower ranking enlisted men in most NATO armies, and rôles requiring any kind of specialised training—including communications and heavy weapons operation—are filled by an NCO. Conversely, because the NCOs are not professional, and lack broad experience or leadership skills, many leadership rôles that would be undertaken by NCOs in NATO armies are undertaken by officers in the Soviet Ground Forces. The Soviets seem to have tried to ameliorate this problem in the late 1970s through a warrant officers' programme, but

this does not appear to have been entirely successful. NCOs make up about a third of the personnel in the Soviet Ground Forces, a somewhat larger fraction than in most NATO armies.

The reason that so few NCOs remain in service is mainly the low pay and low status. A typical junior sergeant's pay of 11.80 rubles monthly is hardly enough for his own needs, and certainly not enough to support a family. In contrast, a junior lieutenant receives 220 rubles monthly, plus additional benefits including family housing and a vacation. A young soldier contemplating a professional military career will attempt to join the officers' ranks rather than remaining an NCO. A small fraction, perhaps five per cent of NCOs are extended-service or professional NCOs who receive the rank of *starshina* (sergeant-major).

The stereotypical sergeant-major is an east Ukrainian, Byelorussian, or a rural Russian from some other region who was raised on a collective farm, where the dreariness of life offers little incentive to return to 'Civvy Street'. Soviet peasants do not receive an internal passport which would allow them to travel to the cities seeking work: in this way they are tied to the collective farms almost as effectively as in the days of serfdom. Collective farmers (*khokolznik*) are very poorly paid, even by Soviet standards, making only about half as much as urban factory workers. In some areas of the country, especially in the Caucasus and Central Asia, this is not quite so important since a fair amount of extra money can be made in black market operations. The singular distinction between serving two years as a conscript sergeant, and accepting another three-year tour of extended duty, is that the extended-tour sergeant-majors receive an internal passport, while sergeants serving only their two years of draft duty are obliged to return to their collective farms. This attraction alone entices a small percentage of the sergeants to remain in the service. These sergeant-majors are derisively referred to as *makaroniki* ('macaroni men') due to their penchant for collecting the annual service duty stripes which are worn to show their seniority. This situation may be changing due to changes in the internal passport rules, implemented in 1974.

The rubberised chemical protection suit can be worn as a waterproof rain poncho if necessary.

The Soviet Officer

There is a much larger gap between Soviet officers and enlisted men than in most NATO armies. A Soviet officer's life is very distinct from that led by the NCOs, and the Army tailors the pay and benefits to attract professional officers.

Nevertheless, not all officers are professionals. Some university students go through officers' training courses in school rather than enter the Army as a common conscript. The lowest officer rank, the junior lieutenant, is intended mainly for such short-term officers. This officer's initial tour of duty is from two to five years, and depends upon the circumstances of the enlistment, for example, the branch of service technical specialisation, and details of further training. The career pattern of a professional officer is usually different from that of a junior lieutenant interested in little more than serving his time and getting out of the Army.

The route into the officer ranks for young men intending to make the Army their career varies, but usually starts with a posting to one of the more than 140 officers' schools. The sheer number of these schools is due to the fact that the Soviet officer corps makes up about 15 per cent of the total personnel of the Soviet Army, which is a larger percentage than in most NATO armies. This is due in some degree to the rôle of junior officers in the Soviet Army, which as mentioned earlier, is closer in actual tasks to that of the professional NCOs of NATO armies. Also, a portion of the Soviet officer corps is involved in political control, as *zampolits* (political officers), who have no direct counterparts in NATO armies.

The Soviet officer schools receive candidates from three sources: enlisted men with a secondary education, pre-military schools, and civilian secondary schools. Although it is not officially admitted, the only enlisted men with a good chance of being accepted for officer school are soldiers of Russian origin (or assimilated non-Russians), with a good military record, and preferably members of the Komsomol youth group. Soldiers who have served with political sections of military units are given special preference. Soldiers can apply for officer schools after their first tour of duty so long as they are not more then 23 years old. The test is the same as that given to students leaving secondary school, but soldiers are accepted for the officers' schools automatically on passing the exams. The Soviet officer corps is disproportionately Russian (probably about 85 per cent) and the Soviet hierarchy seems determined to keep it that way.

There are two kinds of pre-military preparatory schools which provide officer candidates. The nine Suvorov schools, first founded in 1943 for the orphans of servicemen killed in the war, provide five to seven years of education for students who enter the school between the ages of ten and 13 years. The school provides a basic secondary education as well as preliminary military training. In the 1960s the schools were expanded to permit older students,

The OP-1 CBR suit can be worn either in long 'coat' configuration, or gathered and fastened about the legs to make a coverall: see also Plate L. It is not airtight, and must be worn over a chemically-treated body stocking; it is uncomfortable to wear, and in hot weather an hour's wear is more than enough to cause heat exhaustion. (Beryl Barnett Jr.)

who had previously completed eight grades of normal civilian schools, to enter the Suvorov schools for the last two years of the courses. The similar Nakhimov schools were also founded during the war, at locations in Tbilisi (Georgia), Leningrad, and Riga (Latvia). Unlike the Suvorov schools, the Nakhimov schools were intended from the outset only to provide two years of education. Students are accepted by competitive examination after completing eight grades of normal civilian education. About 25–33 per cent of applicants are accepted. The Nakhimov and Suvorov schools provide a high quality education, and are very prestigious. Their students are predominantly Russian, with a smattering of Ukrainians, Byelorussians and other minorities. Students of these schools tend to receive the choicest postings to the officers' schools if their records are good. Graduates wear a distinctive insignia throughout their service career, are automatically admitted to officers' school, and are

The VKK-3M pressurised G-suit and associated GSh-4 helmet were the most common fighter pilot flight suits in the days before fully pressurised cockpits, as demonstrated by these MiG-21 pilots. (Sovfoto)

excused from certain entrance exams for later military schooling; they represent the cream of the Soviet officer corps.

Besides these specialised, full-time pre-military schools, the DOSAAF runs about 40 part-time schools. These provide students in the ninth and tenth grades with their NVF pre-induction training, but offer a more concentrated course with better instruction. DOSAAF schools are usually run in association with a particular branch of a service, and students would attend the school on two days a week, receiving 140 hours of instruction over two years (although aviation schools usually require about double that amount). These schools sponsor special military summer camps which give their students further specialised training. A typical DOSAAF pre-military school is the Leninist Komsomol Young Paratroopers School in Ryazan, formed in 1972 and located near the Airborne Command School and 106th Guards Air Assault Division, which provide the teachers. The school offers the normal NVP regulation training as well as basic parachute drill, and parachute jumping from towers and aircraft.

Students from normal civilian secondary schools are also eligible for officers' school. Applicants are usually between 17 and 21 years old, and must pass competitive exams in mathematics, physics and the Russian language. Students who have received a medal or other distinction during secondary education take only one of the tests, which if passed with a grade of 'excellent' admits them to officers' school. Preference is given to students who have been active in the Komsomol or other Communist party organisations, and to students who have distinguished themselves in DOSAAF paramilitary clubs, or in pre-military NVP training. To some extent, the Russian language test can be used to weed out many non-Russians, and to identify the most highly assimilated non-Russians.

Soviet officers' schools are more specialised than military academies in most NATO countries due to the sheer number of schools. While the US Army has a single officer academy (West Point), each branch of the Soviet services will have several of these schools. For example, in the Ground Forces, the Armoured Force branch has eight officers' schools, the Artillery has seven, etc. There are three types of officers' schools.

1: Motor Rifles honour guard, summer parade
2: Armoured crewman, summer off-duty
3: Motor Rifles, summer work dress

A

Motor Rifles, field uniforms:
1: Summer ('fighting load')
2: Lieutenant, summer
3: Summer ('existence load')

B

Camouflaged field dress:
1: Sgt., VDV, new pattern
2: Motor Rifles, old one-piece
3: Motor Rifles, new two-piece

C

VOLSTAD

Motor Rifles, field dress, Afghanistan, 1986:
1: Winter, lightweight, with armour & chest pouches
2: Summer, with new field cap
3: Summer, with hooded jacket

D

1: Military Police field dress
2: Lt., Medical, summer field dress
3: Engineer, summer field dress

E

Armoured Force field dress:
1: Senior Sgt., summer
2: Office cadet, winter
3: Crewman, summer, underwater escape kit

F

Summer service uniforms:
1: Lt., Motor Rifles, shirtsleeve everyday duty dress
2: Junior Sgt., Artillery, parade/walking-out dress
3: Capt., Artillery, parade/walking-out dress

G

Motor Rifles, winter uniforms:
1: Field dress ('fighting load')
2: Capt., work dress
3: Field dress, Afghanistan, 1986

H

Ch 6 - Introducing Multimedia Applications
    for Classroom learning
    > How do multimedia Applications
    support students meaningful learning?

Ch 7. Learning to Use Multimedia tools to
    create Multimedia Projects
    Z How do students Multimedia
    Projects encourage Meaningful Learning

Ch 8 - Learning to Work w images + Sound
    > How Students benefit from
    collection of and Manipulation of
    Sounds + Graphics

Ch 9 - Learning from Student projects: Knowledge as
    Design and the design of Hypermedia
    > Design Principles
    > Teacher Student interaction

Ch 10 - Being a Responsible User of Technology
    in Classrooms
    > Equity of Access

2300 - 1485
2249 - 805

Checking - 36$\frac{17}{}$ - Bal
14 $\underline{05}$ - Aval;

126 $\frac{38}{}$ ¢ - Bal
104 $\frac{88}{}$ ¢ Avail

↑

$ 126.00

150.00
- 75.00
_____
75.00

2 6.35
17.83
1 2.97
+ _____
2 7.13
16.00
_____
731 5 - Done

150.00
150.00
_____
300.00

55.00
20.00
_____
75.

$22.18

Motor Rifles, winter field dress:
1: Lt. Col., fleece cap and coat
2: Lt., BMP battalion, greatcoat
3: Camouflage coveralls

I

VVS flight & working uniforms:
1: MiG 21 pilot, Frontal Aviation
2: MiG 23 pilot, Frontal Aviation
3: Ground crewman, working dress

J

VVS flight suits:
1: Off-season
2: Lightweight, summer
3: Winter

K

Chemical protective suits:
1,3: OP-1, Combined Arms
2: L-1, Chemical Recce Troops

ЗАРАЖЕНО

L

The Military Technical Schools (VTU) offer three-year courses which train officers in basic tactical skills for specific types of units; there were about 70 of these schools at one time, but they are gradually being upgraded to higher military schools.

The two primary types of officers' schools are the Higher Command Schools (VKU) and the Higher Engineering Schools (VIU). The Higher Command Schools, of which there are about 78, are the most common type. These offer four-year courses with about 60 per cent of the time devoted to specialised military subjects, 30 per cent to academic subjects (including mathematics, physics and foreign language), and 10 per cent to political education. At least six weeks each year are spent training with a line unit from the appropriate branch of service. The Higher Engineering Schools (VIU) are smaller in number, totalling about 26, and offer a more technical education. The curriculum lasts five years, and places greater stress on engineering, mathematics, physics and other technical subjects. Each branch has a mixture of both command and engineering schools. For example, seven out of the Armoured Forces' eight schools are command schools, and one is an engineering school. The command schools provide officers who will lead tactical units in the field, while the engineering schools tend to provide the staff of research establishments, technical services and the defence procurement bureaucracy.

Soviet officers are assigned on graduation to a staff or command position. They may later attend further military educational institutions if their performance warrants it. Advanced courses are offered, taking up to 11 months time, and officers are later eligible for entrance into the military academies. In the USSR, the term 'military academies' is reserved for higher officer training institutions which train officers for command and higher staff positions. There are about 20 such academies, each branch having one or two. There are three types of academies: command, technical and mixed command/technical. The most prestigious is the Military Academy of the General Staff, formerly called the Voroshilov Academy, which trains colonels or major-generals for high staff postings. The academies offer three- to five-year

The VKK suit, worn by crews of newer aircraft with pressurised cockpits like the Sukhoi Su-22. These Sukhoi pilots also wear the ZSh-1M helmet, which—unlike the earlier GSh-4—has integral communications. (Sovfoto)

courses, and are an essential step in the training of all senior officers.

The career of a military officer in the USSR is attractive in terms of salary, status and benefits. A junior lieutenant earns about 220 rubles monthly, and a captain about 250, compared to a factory foreman (supervising 30 men) who receives only 140–160 rubles. Officers' salaries are perhaps a little lower than those of civilians with comparable education; but officers receive other benefits, such as the special *voyentorg* stores which give officers access to goods that are hard to find in the civilian economy. Officers' pension benefits are better on average than those in the civil sector, and medical care is often as good or better. The quality of officer housing varies, but no more than in the civil sector. One drawback of service life, however, is that many

A special lightweight tropical flight uniform was introduced for crews in the southern USSR, like these MiG-23 pilots in the Odessa Military District; it comes in either pale blue, or a pale orange shade. (Sovfoto)

Soviet units are stationed on the periphery of the vast Soviet mainland, far from towns or cities of any size, and this can lead to considerable isolation and hardship for the officers and their families. This is not only the case with the Ground Forces; indeed, probably the most unattractive postings are those of the prestigious Strategic Missile Force, whose silos are located in some of the most god-forsaken reaches of the USSR.

A Soviet officer's career is not significantly different from that in most NATO armies. Efficiency reports (*attestatsiy*) are a regular feature of life, as is the usual process of 'ticket punching' for career advancement. Soviet officers tend to remain in a particular post longer than in the US Army, and there is a more formalised career path alternating between command and staff positions, especially for line officers. Although the Soviets had an 'up-or-out' promotion policy similar to that in the US Army, this is now less vigorously pursued. Soviet regulations permit officers to remain in the service at a particular rank longer than would be the practice in most NATO armies; for example, in the Soviet Army the maximum age for a lieutenant is 40, and the maximum age for majors is 50.

*   *   *

Women in the Army
Although women are not drafted into the Army, women do serve in most of the services in small numbers. They are most common in clerical or medical postings and number only a few tens of thousands. Since the majority of doctors in the USSR are women, it is natural to find them in medical postings in the Army; but Soviet society does not encourage any further expansion of women's military rôles, despite the notable instances of women serving in various combat posts in the Second World War. By the end of the Great Patriotic War, indeed, about a tenth of the Red Army was made up of women, including tank drivers, tank commanders, mortar crews, snipers and pilots, as well as medics and traffic controllers. Although a reversion to this situation is unlikely, current demographic trends may force the Soviet government to encourage more Russian women to enter the services.

Reserve Duty

Once mustered out of the services, Soviet recruits retain a reserve obligation until the age of 50. Soviet reserve personnel are unlike those in most NATO armies in that they have no further training obligations and are unlikely to be recalled to service except in time of war. On rare occasions some reserves have been called up: in the 1968 Czechoslovakia crisis, during the Polish crisis in the early 1980s, in 1979 when Afghanistan was invaded and in 1986 for the Chernobyl power plant clean-up. However, these call-ups were very restricted in nature, and usually affected only the most recent draft years.

Soviet Army Uniforms

The basis for contemporary Soviet Army military uniforms has been the uniform reforms of 1943 and 1969. The 1943 changes revoked many of the Bolshevik innovations in rank insignia, returning to a more traditional Russian, and indeed Tsarist, style. The 1969 reforms did not significantly alter the pattern of insignia and rank, but rather were aimed more at modernising the basic appearance of the uniform; the most noticeable change was the abandonment of the traditional *gimnastyorka* peasant blouse for a more Western style of shirt and jacket, the *rubashka*. Since 1969 the Soviet Army has been undergoing a gradual change in uniforms, spurred in some measure by experience in Afghanistan. Soviet Ground Forces uniforms, while inexpensive and acceptable in a peacetime, garrison army, have been found wanting in combat conditions. The traditional *pilotka* side cap is useless as a field cap, and is being replaced by a forage cap. The field blouse does not have enough pockets, and so is being modified to more closely resemble the Polish and Czechoslovak field blouse. The short field jacket is taking on the appearance of the northern tier Warsaw Pact armies, with a 'fish fur' collar and shoulder pockets. These changes have not yet been formalised in any published uniform orders, but this is likely to occur in the next few years.

The Soviet Army's military dress is fairly uniform between all four branches of the service, except for the Air Forces which, not surprisingly, tend to have a distinctive appearance. Air Force parade

A soldier in Afghanistan, showing the 'Field' branch-of-service collar tabs—here, of a Motor Rifle unit. The Model 40 helmet has the initial style of chin strap.

uniforms tend to favour blue in place of the traditional olive of the other services. However, Soviet Air Force everyday dress follows the same general guidelines as the rest of the Soviet Army except for insignia. Soviet military dress codes identify four basic classes of military uniforms (*forma odyezhda voyenna*):

Paradno-vikhodnaya odyezhda: Parade-Walking Out Dress

Povsednevnaya odyezhda (dlya/vnye stroyu): Everyday Dress (On/Off Duty)

Polevaya odyezhda: Field Dress

Rabochaya odyezhda: Work Dress

Soviet uniform regulations also break down all four classes into two types: *letnyaya* (summer) and *zimnaya* (winter). The Soviet Army also recognises a special sub-category of uniforms for use in the southern regions of the USSR, called *oblegyennaya* (lightweight), although this is often called a tropical uniform in the West. The Soviet Air Forces use the same two basic climatic terms, but add an additional one—*demisezonnaya*—which refers to uniforms worn during the cooler months of the spring and autumn. Although this type is not yet recognised in the other branches, it would appear that the Ground Forces are moving in this direction.

Motor Rifleman (left) and soldier from a Motor Transport unit wearing the grey winter greatcoat. Branch badges are worn on red and black left sleeve patches; branch emblems on the collar tabs. The black branch-of-service colour of the Motor Transport troops shows up sharply against the uniform. Again, note red star, in this case solid, on the right hand soldier's helmet. (Sovfoto)

A special Parade/Walking Out Dress is confined to officers. It is worn only on rare, formal occasions, and the Everyday Dress is much more common. Officers' Parade Dress is characterised by the use of a distinctive 'Tsar green' uniform colour in all branches of the services except the Air Forces, which uses royal blue instead. The more formal Parade Dress is characterised by the wearing of high leather boots and a formal clinch belt, and is usually confined to high military occasions such as parades and displays. The somewhat less formal Walking Out Dress dispenses with the boots in favour of shoes, and the belt is deleted; this mode of dress is used, for formal occasions, including non-military occasions such as social gatherings.

Enlisted men and NCOs have a Parade Dress, but it is not as specialised as the officers' and is not the Tsar green colour. This clothing serves in both the Parade and Everyday rôles with a change of insignia and some other details. For example, more formal collar tabs with brass trim are worn on the Parade uniform, and the collar is folded down to permit the wearing of a dress shirt and tie; on the Everyday uniform the collar tabs are without brass trim and the blouse collars are buttoned up. Parade Dress for enlisted men and NCOs is in the normal olive colour like Everyday Dress.

Everyday Dress is the style worn on garrison duty and is the most common uniform worn during peacetime. In all services except the Air Forces it is of an olive colour. It should be noted that although the Soviets officially refer to the basic uniform colour as 'olive', the shade varies quite a bit, and is closer to what would be called 'khaki' in Britain or 'olive drab' in the United States. There are certain small differences between the details of officers'

Parade and Everyday Dress, such as the use of collar tabs without brass trim and less elaborate shoulder boards. Two types of Everyday Dress are identified, 'On Duty' and 'Off Duty' which correspond to Parade and Parade/Walking Out in the more formal attire. Everyday (On Duty) dress usually includes the wearing of high black leather boots and a belt. This form of dress is standard while the officer or enlisted man is on base, but not involved in any form of field training or work. Everyday (Off Duty), sometimes called Everyday Walking Out Dress, employs much the same clothing, but as in the case of Parade/Walking Out Dress the boots and belt are dispensed with, and normal shoes are worn. As the term implies, this is the standard form of dress when not on duty. In actuality, enlisted men normally wear their field or work uniform while off-duty. Everyday (Off Duty) wear for enlisted men and NCOs is usually reserved for special occasions and only worn where a smart impression is required, for example when visiting a local town, or when off-duty in a major city.

Field Dress is the subject of most of the plates illustrated and refers to the clothing used by Soviet troops for tactical training and for combat. While of similar cut and appearance to Everyday Dress, it is shorn of much of its decorative aspects. For example, in the case of officers, the Field Dress trousers do not carry the branch-of-service colour trim; the shoulder boards and collar tabs are subdued, and a different peaked cap is worn, in subdued colours without the branch-of-service colour band or trim. In the case of enlisted men and NCOs, the shoulder boards remain in the branch colour, and the coloured collar tabs are used. One of the reforms, possibly introduced due to experience in Afghanistan, was the decision to use subdued shoulder boards and collar tabs for enlisted men to reduce their visibility. This is only now beginning to be extended into the USSR itself. Although there is a formal category of Work Dress, these uniforms are not usually in any way distinctive. For the average motor rifleman or tanker the Field and Work uniforms are the same, even though an older and more faded field uniform may be retained for especially filthy chores. Although most are made of an olive fabric, some troops have more specialised Field and Work uniforms of other colours and cuts. The best-known example is the tankers' uniform,

The style of fleece cap issued to female personnel in the Army and Navy (as this example) for winter wear, here modelled by a warrant officer.

which includes both a black coverall for summer and a black short jacket for winter. Other specialised Field and Work uniforms include the wide variety of aircrew uniforms, and the dark blue coveralls of the Strategic Missile Force. There are some specific Work uniforms for certain tasks; for example, troops working in field bakeries wear a white smock and a white beret when at the field ovens.

The Soviet Army is not well known for its close adherence to dress regulations, particularly in the case of enlisted personnel. Part of the problem is simply that the enlisted troops have a minimal selection of personal clothing and, unlike the officers', this clothing does not satisfy the full range of formal dress codes. For example, most troops have only a single winter greatcoat. According to the regulations the greatcoat, when worn as Everyday Dress, is to be decorated with coloured shoulder boards, and the branch-of-service patch on the left sleeve; but when it is worn as Field Dress, these insignia are supposed to be removed. It is impractical to remove these insignia from day to day, so Soviet enlisted troops are often seen in field exercises wearing coats decorated in the nominally incorrect 'Everyday Dress' style. This laxity is further complicated by recent trends to experiment with new types and styles of field clothing which have different patterns of insignia and markings from the 1969 regulations.

The Soviet Army has a penchant for medals and decorations. Troops are regularly awarded distinctions for passing various courses and qualifications or for distinguished service, and these are recognised in the form of small, coloured metal badges, usually worn on the right breast. Certain other badges showing affiliation to Communist Party organisations are also permitted, e.g. the Komsomol pin. Officers tend to collect an even gaudier selection of distinctions, as well as associated ribbons worn on the left breast. These

Lt. Vitaly Akulov, commanding a BMP-1 Motor Rifle platoon, briefs his men during winter field exercises in February 1975 in the Siberian Military District. At left are the squad machine gunner with an RPK and the grenadier with an RPG-7 (evident by the PGO-7 sight case on his belt). At extreme right we see a fairly complete 'existence load' including canteen, rucksack, and shelter-quarter. Akulov wears a tanker's helmet so that he can link in with the BMP's intercom when inside the vehicle; normally he would replace this with a *ushanka* or a steel helmet for dismounted combat. The troops all wear the winter 'fish fur' *ushanka* of enlisted men's quality. (Sovfoto)

various decorations are worn on Parade and Everyday uniforms, and it is not uncommon to see certain types worn even in the field, such as parachute qualification badges or guards regimental insignia. Owing to the sheer volume of these awards, only a few of the more common styles are shown in the accompanying illustrations and photos.

Branch Insignia

Soviet troops wear an elaborate system of branch insignia which vary in detail depending on the degree of formality of the uniform. Branch insignia of the various types are based around a branch colour, the most common colour being red, owing to the fact that it is used by the most numerous type of regiment, the Motor Rifle regiments. Red is also used by the Military Bands and Orchestra of the Ground Forces. The next most common branch colour is black, used by Tank, Artillery, Engineer, Signals and Chemical Defence units as well as various support units including Pipeline Construction, Motor Transport, Rail and River Transport and Topographical. The semi-autonomous VDV Airborne Assault Force uses pale medium blue, as do the few remaining ceremonial Cavalry units. Magenta is used mainly by administrative units including Administration, Medical, Veterinary and Legal units, but it is in the process of being replaced by red. Special security units have their own colours, the KGB using royal blue for its security forces, red for officers of the Kremlin Guard and green for its Border Guards; the MVD uses brown for its internal security troops.

The branch colours are most prominent on Parade and Everyday Dress. On the peaked cap the band and trim is in branch colours. The collar tabs are in branch colour, as are the shoulder boards of enlisted men. The branch-of-service shoulder patch is also backed in the appropriate colour. A distinction should be noted in the use of colours in the case of combined arms units: for example, tankers belonging to a tank company attached to a motor rifle regiment wear the red insignia of the Motor Rifle troops, not the black of the Tank Force.

Besides the colours, the soldier's branch of service or trade is shown in the form of a small branch emblem worn on the collar tab, and also carried on the officers' shoulder boards when in shirtsleeve

Reconnaissance squad members are given instructions by Sr.Lt. A. Rybenok during summer exercises in Siberia, August 1979. All wear standard KLMK camouflage coveralls in grass-green and sand-khaki, with the hood pulled up over the helmet. (Sovfoto)

order. There are over twenty of these emblems, and they are shown in the accompanying illustrations. A form of this insignia is also incorporated into the arm badge worn on Parade and Everyday uniforms. These badges are normally worn only on the left shoulder, but there has been a noticeable trend over the past few years to wear them on both arms. The badge is made of coloured felt with the associated branch and national insignia thermally molded on in a thin layer of yellow and red plastic. This is different from the usual style of woven insignia used in Western Europe, and even in much of the rest of the Warsaw Pact. These patches are shown in the accompanying illustrations. It should be noted that the Motor Rifle arm badge design is also used for KGB and Interior Army troops, but

Jr.Sgt. A. Torosyan and his T-55A(M) tank crew during September 1984 exercises in the Odessa Military District. There has been an increasing tendency to stencil white numbers on the left leg pocket and left sleeve of tank coveralls, as here, but the significance of these numbers is unexplained. (Sovfoto)

the cloth background is in the appropriate branch colour, not red.

Shoulder boards were re-established in 1943, and are worn on most uniforms except for Field Dress (and can even been seen there, contrary to regulations). The enlisted man's shoulder board is in the branch colour, most commonly red (Motor Rifle) or black (Tank, Artillery), with the cyrillic letters 'CA' (*Sovietskaya Armiya*). There is some confusion about the use of the 'CA' cypher; the original 1969 regulations envisioned using it only on the Parade uniform, but they have since become ubiquitous and are seen on Everyday and even Field Dress. Non-commissioned officers' ranks are superimposed on these shoulder boards. There are at least three distinctly different styles of officers' shoulder boards; an elaborate and colourful Parade shoulder board, a subdued Everyday version, and a smaller shirtsleeve-order subdued shoulder board.

Soviet Military Headdress

The peaked cap is issued to all troops, though its use is most popularly associated with officers who wear it even in the field. It is sometimes referred to derisively in units as the 'SS cap' due to the association of something resembling this shape with the Germans. Officers have three peaked caps: a Parade cap, in Tsar green (or dark blue for Air Force); an Everyday cap, with branch-of-service coloured band and trim; and a cap in subdued colours for use in Field or Work Dress. The enlisted men receive only a single peaked cap, worn for Parade or Walking Out, which is similar to the officers' Everyday peaked cap—in the basic olive colour, with branch-of-service coloured band and trim. This cap is rarely worn by enlisted personnel, hence its association with officers.

The cap more commonly associated with NCOs and enlisted men is the *pilotka* sidecap. This is the standard Everyday, Field and Work cap. In southern climes it is replaced by the brimmed, circular sun hat. In 1984 the Limited Soviet Contingent in Afghanistan began issuing a new forage cap to replace the *pilotka*: it would appear that this will be worn by both enlisted men and officers. The *pilotka* is supplemented with a variety of berets in various branches of the service. The Tank Force wears a black beret, and the VDV Air Assault Force wears a medium/pale blue version. The Strategic Missile Force wears a dark blue beret, and berets are also worn as work caps in some trades, such as bakers and Air Force ground crewmen.

The most common form of winter wear is the traditional Russian *ushanka* fur cap. It comes in a better grade for officers, and the enlisted man's cap is made from a synthetic material, commonly called 'fish fur' in Russia. Regimental officers and above wear the *papakha*, a high fur cap. The national insignia worn on these caps varies in detail from enlisted men to officers.

The Soviet Army uses two types of steel combat helmet. The most common style is the Second World War vintage Model 1940, which has been improved upon on a number of occasions, mainly in terms of helmet liners and chin straps. There are two common chin strap variations, one of a 'V' shape, the other a conventional belt. It is believed that this helmet is now designated the SSh-40 and SSh-40m, but this is not certain. The Soviet Army has introduced a newer helmet, the SSh-60, which has a slightly higher crown, and is distinctive due to the more pronounced angle of the front of the helmet when compared with the more rounded Model 1940. This helmet may eventually replace the Model 1940, although the Soviet Army appears to be in no rush to do so. Although helmet nets were not unheard of prior to 1980, they were uncommon. Recent experience in Afghanistan has led to more interest in this feature, which is becoming more common. There is a version with simulated fabric foliage attached; and in Afghanistan and the southern USSR some units have been seen wearing helmet covers of a light khaki or camouflage pattern fabric.

Besides the basic steel helmet, there are a variety of protective helmets worn by specialised troops. The best known of these is the tankers' padded cloth helmet, patterned after the wartime design but with earflaps reconfigured to accommodate the improved intercom system contained in the helmet. Although it is most commonly used by armoured vehicle crews, it is also worn by certain other

The standard summer tankers' helmet is similar to the Second World War version but has different ear guards for the intercom. Note the quick-attachment jack for the intercom system. (Author's photo)

specialised troops, such as tactical missile launcher crews; in some of these cases the tank intercom equipment is removed. The VDV airborne force has also been adopting a modified version of this helmet without the ear guards for the intercom equipment. A winter version of this helmet is also produced, which has a 'fish fur' lining. Aircrews have a variety of specialised helmets, many of the more common types being shown in the accompanying illustrations.

Camouflage Uniforms

The Soviet Army has used a variety of camouflage uniforms over the past decades, but since the late 1960s, has standardised on a single pattern of fabric. This is in a medium green with small, angular splotches of pale khaki. The most common form of camouflage dress is a simple coverall, the KLMK (*kamuflirovanniy letniy maskirovochniy kombinezon*). The

KLMK was initially issued on a very restricted basis and was intended mainly for snipers: it even came with an accompanying facemask of the same fabric as the coveralls. In the 1980s distribution of the KLMK has increased considerably, to the point where entire motor rifle units have been so fitted. The Soviet KGB Border Guards have their own variation of this uniform, using the same camouflage material but cut as a more conventional blouse and trousers combination. In the early 1980s the Soviet Ground Forces began to receive a variation of the KLMK made of a coarser-textured material similar to burlap, but printed with the same camouflage pattern. This coarse fabric was probably introduced to provide the garment with improved concealment qualities against newer infra-red sensors. In 1985 the Soviet VDV showed a new pattern of camouflage uniform (see Plate C1), but it is unclear if this will be used outside the airborne branch. Besides these summer camouflage suits, there is a common white winter coverall designed to fit over the normal cold-weather garb.

February 1985: Col. N. I. Sharypa instructs officer candidate I. Stepanshuk on the T-62 tank during field exercises at Omsk Higher Tank Command School. The 'K' on the shoulder boards of the winter tanker's jacket identifies Stepanshuk's status as an officer cadet—'kursant'.

Accoutrements

Soldiers in the Soviet Ground Forces are provided with a far less extensive variety and supply of field accoutrements and packs than their NATO counterparts. The basic *fighting load* consists of an ersatz-leather belt, a cloth or leather web suspender, an AKM ammunition pouch and a gas mask bag. The AKM pouch is always worn to the right of the belt buckle and the gas mask bag is always slung diagonally over the shoulder, resting on the left hip. If carried, the 6Kh4 or other AK bayonets are usually worn to the immediate left of the belt buckle. On occasion, a small pouch is carried left of the bayonet; this can be either a small cleaning kit for the individual weapon, a pouch for two grenades, or a small medical kit. In bad weather, a field cape/shelter half can be carried, rolled up, on the webbing harness. It is interesting to note that, in most circumstances, the fighting load does not appear to include a canteen or entrenching tool.

For the *existence load*, the fighting load is supplemented by a rucksack; in addition, a canteen is usually carried on the left rear hip, and sometimes an entrenching tool on the right. The standard Soviet pack is very simple and very small by NATO standards. The cape/shelter half can be lashed to

the top of it, and it probably contains food and additional clothing. Very little is known about Soviet heavy existence load-carrying equipment apart from the large rucksack. Soviet troops do not seem to be issued with sleeping bags, and apparently rely on blankets. Heavy existence load equipment seems to be seldom, if ever, used in peacetime, even during exercises. What provisions are required are carried on trucks, or in the armoured personnel carriers; it appears that Soviet field equipment is extremely spartan.

Officers have a fairly standard selection of field accoutrements, the most ubiquitous being a leather map case carried over the right hip, and signal flags (one red, one white), carried in a small cloth holster to the left of the belt buckle. A variety of binoculars is available as well.

Bibliography

There are dozens of recent books, and thousands of articles on the Soviet Army, covering its equipment, weapons, tactics, organisation and doctrine. This short bibliography is by no means comprehensive, but a guide to several of the better general studies on the Soviet Army available on an unclassified basis in English:

William P. Baxter, *Soviet AirLand Battle Tactics*, (Presidio Press, Novato, CA: 1986).

John Erickson & E. J. Feuchtwanger, *Soviet Military Power and Performance*, (Macmillan, London: 1979).

David C. Isby, *Russia's War in Afghanistan, Men-at-Arms No. 178*, (Osprey Publishing, London: 1986).

David C. Isby, *Weapons and Tactics of the Soviet Army*, (Jane's Publishing, London: 1981)

Ellen Jones, *Red Army and Society*, (Allen & Unwin, Boston: 1985).

Alfred L. Monks, *Soviet Military Doctrine: 1960 to the Present*, (Irvington Publishers, NY: 1984).

H. F. Scott & W. F. Scott, *The Armed Forces of the USSR*, (Westview Press, Boulder, Co: 1984).

Viktor Suvorov, *Inside the Soviet Army*, (Hamish Hamilton, London: 1982).

Viktor Suvorov, *The Liberators*, (Hamish Hamilton, London: 1981).

S. J. Zaloga & J. W. Loop. *Elite 5, Soviet Bloc Élite Forces*, (Osprey Publishing, London: 1985).

The Plates

(Since basic uniform practice is covered in the preceding section, most of the following commentaries are limited to brief identification only.)

A1: Motor Rifleman, Honour Guard, Summer Parade Dress
The most formal category of uniform worn by enlisted men. Note winged national insignia on cap, peculiar to Parade Dress.

A2: Crewman, Armoured Force, Summer Everyday (Off Duty) Dress
Note simpler national insignia on cap, and trousers worn loose over shoes.

A3: Motor Rifleman, Summer Work Dress
The most common uniform of the enlisted man; Work Dress is usually of a cheaper material than Field Dress, and fades to a pale khaki.

B1: Motor Rifleman, Summer Field Dress, Fighting Load
Basic tactical uniform and kit, worn for training and combat, with Model 40 helmet. Fighting load consists of belt, load webbing, gas mask haversack, decontamination or medical kit (left of buckle), 6Kh4 bayonet, and magazine pouch for AK-74.

This black leather, pile-collared version of the Soviet tanker's vehicle uniform seems mainly to be worn for parades, but is seen occasionally in the field. These BMP-2 crewmen photographed during the November 1985 Moscow parade wear yellow and red Motor Rifles shoulder boards, and branch patches on both sleeves.

One of the more common roles for the small number of women in the Soviet Army is as medics; here Warrant Officer Irena Sukova is seen wearing Field Dress, with subdued Artillery and Rocket Force collar tabs and shoulder boards, and drab field beret. She also wears the red Komsomol pin; and carries a standard medical kit.

B2: Lieutenant, Motor Rifles, Summer Field Dress
The field peaked cap is often worn instead of the issue helmet by officers as a distinguishing feature. Note subdued insignia; officers' Sam Browne belt, with holstered Makarov pistol (an assault rifle may be carried); map case; and, here, the monocular image intensification night vision device. Issue of expensive night vision devices is on a lower scale than in NATO armies, and monoculars are preferred to binocular face-mask types.

B3: Motor Rifleman, Summer Field Dress, Existence Load
Note SSh-60 helmet, and RPK-74 squad automatic. The existence load differs from the fighting load in that additional clothing, food, mess implements, and a blanket are carried in the R-45 *ryukzak* (rucksack), and a canteen and entrenching tool are issued. A more extensive load using the larger *ryukzak bolshoi* exists but seems less common.

C1: Sergeant, VDV, Summer Field Dress (camouflaged)
The Airborne Assault Force tends to go its own way,

to some extent, in the matter of uniforms. This new camouflage dress, introduced c.1985, follows the cut of Polish and Czechoslovakian examples. This is rumoured to be in fact a *Spetsnaz*[1] uniform, but this seems unlikely. (According to Viktor Suvorov the *Spetsnaz* has its own field uniform in light grey: a basic jacket and trousers, worn with leather jump boots and jump helmet, plus a winter parka with a detachable extension which can be fitted to the bottom to convert it into a longer greatcoat in extremely cold weather. The *Spetsnaz* also reportedly carry a rucksack derived from the VDV's RD-45 but with modernised webbing.) This paratrooper carries the new RPO launcher, akin to a bazooka, which can fire either high explosive or incendiary rounds and is intended to replace conventional flamethrowers.

C2: Motor Rifleman, Summer Field Dress (camouflaged)
The most common camouflage uniform: the KLMK, in grass green with angular sand splotches. The helmet cover with artificial foliage underlines currently increased Soviet interest in field camouflage. His AK is fitted with an image-intensification (passive) night sight.

C3: Motor Rifleman, Summer Field Dress (camouflaged)
In the mid-1980s this new, two-piece version of the KLMK has been introduced, in a coarse sacking material treated to reduce infra-red visibility. This RPG gunner carries the new RPG-16; when not in use the openings of the launch tube are covered and the PGO-16 sight is carried in the small pouch on the left of the belt. Note standard RPG grenade back pack.

D1: Motor Rifleman, Lightweight Winter Field Dress;
Afghanistan, 1986
Since 1985 the Limited Contingent of Soviet Forces/Afghanistan has introduced a variety of new uniform items. This new winter jacket, roughly resembling the traditional officers' winter work jacket but with pockets and other features similar to Polish and Czechoslovak equivalents, is replacing the clumsy greatcoat. Experience in Afghanistan has also led to the introduction of a variety of armoured vests, this example being used by road

[1]See Elite 5, *Soviet Bloc Élite Forces*, for further details of airborne and élite forces uniforms.

patrols and truck drivers. Photos taken in Afghanistan in 1986 also show this new chest pouch rig for AK-74 magazines.

D2: Motor Rifleman, Lightweight Summer Field Dress; Afghanistan, 1986

Recent photos show this new outfit, including a forage cap. Unusually, some Motor Rifles troops are shown wearing the striped blue and white undershirt previously limited—as a sign of élite status—to Airborne and Naval infantry forces; could this be a sign of unit distinction earned in combat? Note R-105M manpack radio, which can also be accompanied by an amplifier carried by a second soldier.

D3: Motor Rifleman, Lightweight Summer Field Dress; Afghanistan, 1986

Some Motor Rifle units have been issued the light hooded jacket introduced from 1984, with new gathered trousers, for mountain infantry[2], and wear it over the normal lightweight summer Field Dress. Note LPO-50 flamethrower, in the process of being replaced by the RPO and RPO-A.

E1: Military Police (Commandant Branch) Field Dress

The Commandant (Military Police) and Traffic Regulator branches of the Ground Forces wear similar uniforms: black fabric or black leather versions of normal Field Dress, for summer and winter respectively. For traffic duty a chest reflector is worn, with white/pale blue/red belts and arm bands. Commandant troops wear a 'K' insignia on the left shoulder; Traffic Regulators, a Cyrillic 'R' (Roman 'P'). Simple painted batons are used for directing traffic.

E2: Lieutenant, Medical and Veterinary Services, Summer Field Dress

Standard women's Field Dress, with standard field medical kit. Male medics carry weapons, but not—so far—female personnel.

E3: Engineer, Summer Field Dress

The jerkin traditional to this branch has been misidentified in some Western publications as body armour. Leather and padded winter versions are

Although it is not often seen, the Soviet Army does issue a large rucksack—*ryukzak bolshoi*—of olive drab fabric, with brown leather reinforced edging and black leather straps. (Beryl Barnett Jr.)

known. The IMP mine detector has failed to impress US soldiers who have tested it: they report that it would be difficult to find a metal chair in an empty room if relying on the IMP's sensitivity!

F1: Senior Sergeant, Armoured Force, Summer Field Dress

Standard black coveralls, and the black beret used by Armoured Force personnel in place of the *pilotka* or new forage cap (though some units still wear the *pilotka*). The unexplained white '1' in a diamond on the left sleeve may perhaps refer to crew seniority. Red and white signal flags are still regularly used during periods of radio silence. The AKSU (sometimes called the AKR) is a short carbine version of the AK-74 used by vehicle crews.

F2: Officer Cadet, Armoured Force, Winter Field Dress

The jacket is worn over padded coveralls in extremely cold weather. The PNV-57 night vision binoculars are usually worn by vehicle drivers in lieu of normal metascope or image-intensification periscopes in the vehicles.

[2]See Elite 5, Plate B3.

F3: Crewman, Armoured Force, Summer Field Dress and IP-46 underwater evacuation gear

The special OPVT kit permits Soviet tanks to be driven underwater for rapid crossing of natural barriers in combat. This is a difficult procedure: even 40-ton tanks retain some buoyancy, having a very uncertain footing on riverbeds, and in case of stranding crews are issued this rebreathing apparatus. The rubber mask is placed over the head; then the tank is slowly flooded until the hatches can be opened, and the crew swim to the surface.

(Crews are also normally issued life jackets, though the author finds it hard to believe that anyone could get out of a hatch wearing this apparatus and an inflated life jacket.) The helmet bears the tank's number: 2nd battalion, 6th company (of a nine-company regiment), 3rd tank.

G1: Lieutenant, Motor Rifles, Summer Everyday Dress (On Duty, Shirtsleeve Order)

Commonly worn in hot weather, when performing administrative or similar chores, this dress order has its own smaller, lighter, subdued-colour shoulder boards.

G2: Junior Sergeant, Artillery, Summer Parade/Walking Out Dress

Worn on formal occasions, such as social functions

Officers of the M. V. Frunze Academy under instruction from Col. Vladimir Zubarev during February 1980 field training. Zubarev wears the *obchina,* **and the high** *papahka* **fleece cap authorised only for more senior professional officers. Maj. Vasili Sviridov (left) carries a large staff map case; more compact cases are carried in the field by junior officers. (Sovfoto)**

at the base, this female NCO's dress order is in the same 'Tsar green' as officers' parade uniform.

G3: Captain, Artillery, Summer Parade/Walking Out Dress
Described in the body of the text, this 'Tsar green' dress order is reserved for special functions and would not be worn for everyday duty.

H1: Motor Rifleman, Winter Field Dress, Fighting Load
The enlisted man's traditional long greatcoat, of coarse fabric or wool, is officially dark grey, but in practice varies from mid-grey to dark green. The use of Everyday uniform distinctions on this coat in the field is explained in the text. Note AK-74 fitted with BG-15 grenade launcher.

H2: Captain, Motor Rifles, Winter Work Dress
Officers are issued this short jacket as a winter work coat; quite popular, it is sometimes worn in place of the greatcoat when the weather permits. It is fairly typical of the Ground Forces' trend towards the category of dress termed in the Air Forces *demisezonnaya*, meaning uniforms intended for wear in spring and autumn.

H3: Motor Rifleman, Winter Field Dress, 1986
This new enlisted men's short winter jacket has begun to appear in Afghanistan. As well as his AK-74 this rifleman carries a slung RPG-18—a 'use once and throw away' tube, copied from the US LAW anti-tank rocket, and designed to supplement the reloadable RPG-16.

I1: Lieutenant-Colonel, Motor Rifles, Winter Field Dress
Sheepskin coats are common winter wear among Soviet officers; enlisted men are usually only issued them in areas of arctic cold. Note officer's *ushanka*; these are usually of real fur or fleece, while the enlisted men's are made of synthetic 'fish fur'.

I2: Lieutenant, Motor Rifles, Winter Field Dress
This platoon commander wears the simple greatcoat most commonly seen among junior officers. The tanker's helmet is characteristic of BMP units, enabling the officer to communicate with the vehicle crew, but would be replaced with a helmet in actual combat outside the APC. Note PSM pistol.

A Motor Rifle senior lieutenant wearing the new raincoat introduced for officers during the 1969 uniform reforms, with Everyday Dress. (Sovfoto)

I3: Motor Rifleman, Winter Field Dress
The winter camouflage coveralls are worn over normal winter field dress. In combat situations coloured arm bands would be worn to distinguish friend from foe, the exact configuration being changed daily for security reasons. Some MR units in northern regions are trained to fight from skis, often having the special MT-LBV arctic armoured transporter instead of the usual BTR-60/70 or BMP.

J1: MiG-21 pilot, VVS Frontal Aviation
The VKK-3M G-suit is common among crews of older aircraft such as the MiG-21, or other high performance types which do not have fully pressurised cabins. It is worn with the GSh-4 helmet, allowing it to be hermetically sealed. The blue webbing presumably contains personal survival equipment.

MiG-27 pilots based in the Transbaikal Military District in February 1979 wearing the heavier coveralls and flight jacket worn over the G-suit in winter. (Sovfoto)

J2: MiG-23 pilot, VVS Frontal Aviation
This new VKK G-suit is replacing the older VKK-3M among pilots of more modern aircraft with pressurised cockpits, such as the MiG-23 and Su-22. It is worn with the more comfortable ZSh-1M or ZSh-3 helmets, and KM-32 or equivalent face masks.

J3: VVS ground crewman, Work Dress
The black jacket and trousers and the beret are traditional ground crew dress. A new lightweight summer alternative has been introduced in the 1980s: a loose jacket and trousers, worn without a shirt but with a beret, in a pale sand-khaki. The suit is broadly similar to the flight suit shown as Plate K2.

K1: VVS Off-Season Flight Suit
For colder weather, especially in aircraft without cabin pressurisation, or temperature controls, this flight jacket and trousers are worn—over the VKK G-suits in fighters, or over normal ground uniforms in transport aircraft, etc. This older ZSh-3 helmet has no integral communications, and is worn over the ShZ-61 leather communications helmet, in black or brown with self-contained earphones. The life jacket is the ASZh model.

K2: VVS Lightweight Summer Flight Suit
Loose-fitting, for wear over G-suits if necessary, this suit comes in either light blue or this stone shade.

K3: VVS Winter Flight Suit
For particularly cold conditions this suit is worn—here, with only the ShZ-61 communications helmet, a practice so common among helicopter

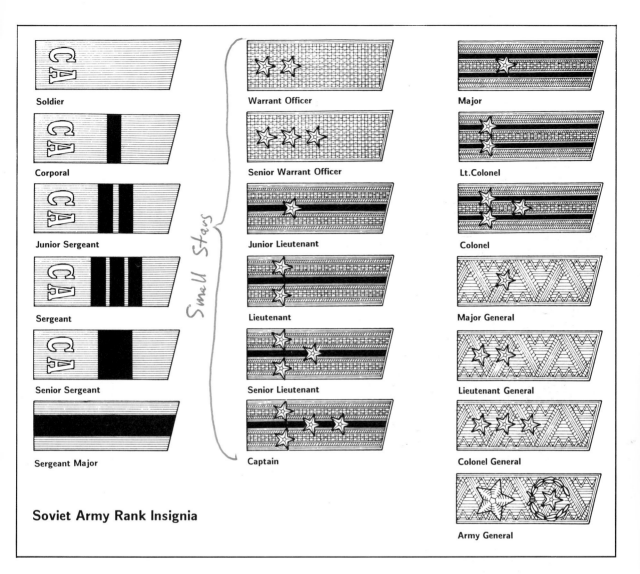

Soldier

Corporal

Junior Sergeant

Sergeant

Senior Sergeant

Sergeant Major

Warrant Officer

Senior Warrant Officer

Junior Lieutenant

Lieutenant

Senior Lieutenant

Captain

Small Stars

Major

Lt.Colonel

Colonel

Major General

Lieutenant General

Colonel General

Army General

Soviet Army Rank Insignia

pilots that the ShZ-61 has frequently been misidentified as a helicopter crew helmet. There is another special arctic flight suit for the most extreme conditions, worn mainly by crews of older transport aircraft with inadequate cabin heating.

Russian rank titles are (*top to bottom, left column*): **Ryadovoi, Yefreitor, Mladshiy serzhant, Serzhant, Starshiy serzhant, Starshina;** (*top to bottom, centre column*): **Praporshchik, Starshiy praporshchik, Mladshiy leytenant, Leytenant, Starshiy leytenant, Kapitan;** (*top to bottom, right column*): **Mayor, Podpolkovnik, Polkovnik, General mayor, General leytenant, General polkovnik, General armii.**

L1, L3: OP-1 Combined Arms Chemical Protective Suit
Currently the most common form of such protective clothing in the Ground Forces, the OP-1 is designed to be worn long, as in L3, or gathered up and strapped into a coverall, as in L1. Soviet troops normally carry only a gas mask and a chemically impregnated paper sheet which folds out into a small tent, providing limited protection until the suit can be donned. The suit is usually carried rolled up on the straps of the fighting load harness or at the top of the rucksack. It is not hermetically sealed, so

the wearer must first put on a chemically impregnated grey cloth body stocking. The suit is of rubberised fabric, without ventilation, and can only be worn for less than an hour in warm, strenuous conditions before the wearer collapses from heat exhaustion. Colours vary from a kind of orange to pale green.

L1 wears the basic enlisted men's ShM mask, hermetically sealed and extremely uncomfortable. L3, an officer, wears the ShM Model K, with a small voice device which allows officers and NCOs to speak to troops. Neither model has any means for drinking liquid. The soldier L1 wears three-finger winter protective gloves, and L3 the five-finger black summer protective gloves. In comparison to current NATO issue, especially the British-developed types with semi-permeable charcoal impregnated fabric, Soviet suits are primitive, uncomfortable, and dangerous to wear over prolonged periods.

L1 carries a standard chemical detection kit, the VPKhR; hand-operated, this can be used to test soil samples. On the ground is a GSP-1M automatic chemical agent detector-alarm. This tests for common G-type nerve agents, and has a secondary function of alerting for radioactive contamination. The officer L3 uses the PPKhR hand-held chemical

detector, semi-automatic and powered off the batteries of a chemical scout vehicle such as the BRDM-2Rkhb.

L2: L-1 Chemical Reconnaissance Troops Chemical Suit
A multi-piece suit issued mainly to Chemical Defence Force personnel, the L1 is more thoroughly sealed against air intrusion. This ShMS mask differs from the others in that it can be fitted with optically corrected lenses which substitute for eyeglasses when the mask is worn. Made of optical glass, they allow the wearer to operate optical sights, and the mask is issued to gun crews, tank gunners, RPG-7 gunners, etc. This man carries a DP-12 contamination survey meter to check for radioactive contamination. In the background is a typical Soviet contamination sign, which is planted by a marking system on the rear of BRDM-2Rkhb chemical scout vehicles.

The background colours of these left-sleeve branch-of-service patches are described in the text.

Motor Rifle	Artillery	Armoured	Air Force	Air Assault	Engineers
Chemical Defence	Motor Transport	Railway Transport	Signals	Pipeline	Construction
Topographical	Technical Schools	Bands	Medical	Kremlin Guards Officers	Commandant Service

Soviet Army Shoulder Badges

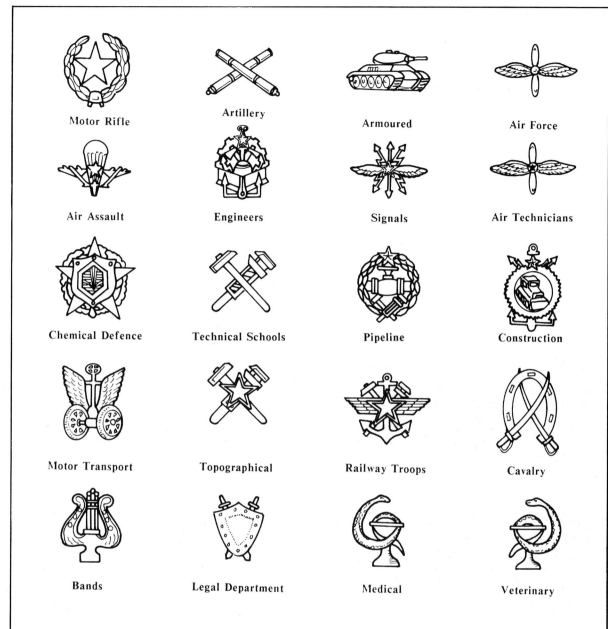

Motor Rifle

Artillery

Armoured

Air Force

Air Assault

Engineers

Signals

Air Technicians

Chemical Defence

Technical Schools

Pipeline

Construction

Motor Transport

Topographical

Railway Troops

Cavalry

Bands

Legal Department

Medical

Veterinary

Soviet Army Branch Emblems

Notes sur les planches en couleur

A1 L'uniforme le plus conventionnel porté par les troupes ordinaires; notez l'insigne national sur le képi—ce style est particulier à la tenue de parade. **A2** Notez l'insigne national plus simple; et les pantalons tombants sur les chaussures. **A3** Toile moins coûteuse, se décolorant à un ton plus clair.

B1 Tenue d'instruction et de combat avec le casque *M40*; remarquez l'équipement de combat, avec ceinture, bretelles, sac à masque à gaz, sacs à munition et ensemble de décontamination, *AK-74* et bayonnette. **B2** Notez le képi de cet officier d'une qualité pour campagne. Il peut porter un fusil ainsi qu'un pistolet *Makarov*. Il tient à la main un dispositif de vision nocturne monoculaire. **B3** Notez le casque *SSh-60*; arme automatique légère *RPK-74*; et sac à dos *R-45*, gamelle et outil de tranchée, avec 'équipement de subsistance'.

C1 Notez le style nouveau de l'uniforme de camouflage, qui est apparu parmi les troupes aéroportées vers l'année 1985. Le *RPO* est un lanceur d'explosifs à grande puissance ou de projectiles incendiaires. **C2** La *KLMK*, combinaison réglementaire de camouflage d'une pièce. **C3** Nouvel uniforme de camouflage de deux pièces en grosse toile brute qui réduirait apparemment sa visibilité à l'infrarouge. Notez le nouveau lanceur *RPG-16*, ses visées étant transportées dans un sac sur le côté gauche de la ceinture.

D1 Nouvelle veste d'hiver, semblable à la veste de travail des officiers qui commence maintenant à remplacer la capote. Notez le gilet de protection et l'emploi des sacs à munition portés sur la poitrine. **D2** Nouvel uniforme complet avec bonnet à pointe de campagne; et chose étrange, le maillot à rayures qui était auparavant particulier aux troupes navales et aéroportées. **D3** Veste légère avec capuche, telle qu'elle était portée par les troupes en montagne mais distribuée maintenant plus largement; notez aussi le lance-flammes *LPO-50*.

E1 Des uniformes de toile noire ou de cuir sont aussi portés par ce service, avec ces embellissements colorés pour des missions de contrôle de la circulation. **E2** Uniforme féminin, réglementaire de campagne; bien que le personnel médical masculin ne porte des armes les femmes n'en portent pas. **E3** Ce gilet n'est pas un justaucorps de protection; c'est un justaucorps, de cuir ou de toile rembourré. Le détecteur de mines *IMP* n'est pas très sensible.

F1 Des bérets noirs sont portés parfois au lieu du *pilotka* par les équipages des chars. Il n'y a pas d'explication au chiffre '1' dans un diamant. La carabine est un *AKSU*. **F2** Veste d'hiver portée sur combinaison rembourrée; notez aussi les jumelles de vision nocturne *PNV-57*. **F3** Dispositif étanche de fuite sous-marine pour les équipages des chars mis hors de combat alors qu'ils traversent des fleuves.

G1 Cet uniforme, pour les tâches administratives quotidiennes en été, a un style qui lui est propre de bordures d'épaules plus petites de couleur sobre. **G2** Uniforme 'vert tsar' porté par le personnel féminin lors de cérémonies formelles. **G3** Uniforme de cérémonie spécial, 'vert Tsar' pour les officiers.

H1 La couleur de la capote varie de gris moyen à vert foncé. Des photos montrent cet insigne de couleur utilisé en campagne—les soldats n'ont qu'une capote et ajouter et retirer constamment leur insigne est trop ennuyeux. Notez la combinaison fusil/lance-grenades *AK-74/BG-15*. **H2** Notez la veste de travail spéciale des officiers à col de fourrure. **H3** Nouvelle veste de soldat, semblable à celle portée par H2; et notez le nouveau tube lance-roquettes 'jetable'.

I1 Les manteaux en peau de mouton, courants parmi les officiers, ne sont distribués aux soldats que par les températures hivernales les plus extrêmes en Arctique. L'*ushanka* réservée aux officiers est en vraie fourrure ou laine de mouton. **I2** La capote est plus courante pour les officiers subalternes. Le casque d'équipage de véhicule blindé l'identifie comme étant un officier d'une unité *BMP*. **I3** Ces brassards de couleur sont changés chaque jour pour des raisons de sécurité et sont souvent portés avec cette combinaison pour identifier les amis des ennemis.

J1 Combinaison *VKK-3M*, courante parmi les équipages de *MiG-21* par ex., sans cockpit entièrement pressurisé; porté ici avec le casque *GSh-4*. **J2** Cette combinaison se porte dans les cockpits entièrement pressurisés, des *MiG-23*, *Su-22* par ex., avec le casque *ZSh-1M* ou *ZSh-3* et le masque protecteur *KM-32*. **J3** Uniforme de travail pour temps froid pour les équipes au sol.

K1 Tenue de vol pour temps froid portée sur uniformes-*G* dans les cockpits non pressurisés et non chauffés; le casque *ZSh-3* n'a pas d'accessoires de communications et est porté sur le casque en cuir de communications *ShZ-61*. **K2** Fabriqué aussi en bleu clair, pour les combinaisons *G*, si souple qu'on la distingue à peine. **K3** Cette combinaison est caractéristique des pilotes d'hélicoptère par temps froid.

L1, L3 Deux façons de porter la combinaison *OP-1*, distribuée le plus couramment: chaude, lourde à porter et non étanche, il faut la porter sur une 'combinaison d'une pièce' en toile imprégnée d'un produit chimique. Contrairement à L1 qui porte un masque *ShM* cet officier (L3) porte un modèle *ShM Model K*, avec dispositif de radiotéléphonie. **L2** Combinaison plus étanche *L-1* pour les troupes de reconnaisance chimique, avec masque de qualité supérieure *ShMS* avec verres de contact optique. Ces personnages portent des dispositifs de détection de contamination variés.

Farbtafeln

A1 Die am deutlichsten für formelle Anlässe konzipierte Uniform gewöhnlicher Soldaten; man beachte die für Paradeuniformen typischen Nationalfarben auf der Mütze. **A2** Man beachte die einfacheren Nationalfarben und die lose über die Schuhe getragenen Hosen. **A3** Billigeres Material mit einem helleren Farbton.

B1 Im Training und in der Schlacht getragen, mit M40 Helm; man beachte die 'Kampfausrüstung' mit Gürtel, Hosenträgern, Gasmaskenbehälter, Beutel für Munition und Entgiftung, AK-74 und Bajonett. **B2** Man beachte die Feldmütze für Offiziere. Ausser der Makarov-Pistole kann auch ein Gewehr getragen werden. Er hält ein monokulares Nachtsichtgerät. **B3** Man beachte den SSh-60 Helm, die leichte automatische RPK-74 und den R-45 Rucksack, das Kochgeschirr und Grabegerät, die 'Überlebensausrüstung'.

C1 Man beachte die Tarnuniform im neuen Stil, die unter den Luftlandetruppen um 1985 erstmals auftrat. Der RPO ist ein Startgerät für hochexplosive oder Brandgeschosse. **C2** Der KMK, der übliche einteilige Overall mit Tarnmuster. **C3** Neue zweiteilige Tarnuniform aus grobem Material, das offenbar die infrarote Sichtbarkeit reduziert. Man beachte den neuen RPG-16 Starter, dessen Visier in einem Beutel links am Gürtel getragen wird.

D1 Neue Winterjacke, ähnlich der Arbeitsjacke für Offiziere, die jetzt die grossen Mäntel ersetzt. Man beachte die kugelsichere Weste und den Brustbeutel für Munition. **D2** Neue Uniform mit Feldmütze und merkwürdigerweise dem gestriften Unterhemd, das zuvor Marine- und Luftlandesoldaten kennzeichnete. **D3** Leichte Jacke mit Kapuze, zunächst von Bergeinheiten getragen, jetzt aber verbreitet; man beachte den LPO-50 Flammenwerfer.

E1 Uniformen aus schwarzem Stoff oder Leder werden von dieser Waffengattung mit farbigen Aufsätzen für Einsätze bei der Verkehrsregelung getragen. **E2** Die übliche Felduniform für Frauen; im Gegensatz zum männlichen medizinischen Personal tragen die Frauen keine Waffen. **E3** Das Oberhemd ist nicht kugelsicher, es ist eine Jacke aus Leder oder gestepptem Stoff. Der IMP-Minendetektor ist nicht sehr empfindlich.

F1 Schwarze Barrette werden von Panzersoldaten oft anstelle der *pilotka* getragen. Die '1' in einem Diamanten ist bisher nicht identifiziert. Der Karabiner ist ein Modell ASKU. **F2** Winterjacke über gestepptem Overall; man beachte ausserdem das PNV-57 Nachtsicht-Fernrohr. **F3** Unterwasser-Notausrüstung für Panzersoldaten, die über Flüsse waten müssen.

G1 Diese für tägliche Verwaltungsaufgaben im Sommer gedachte Uniform hat ihre eigenen, kleineren Schulterklappen mit gedämpfteren Farben. **G2** Die 'zarengrüne' Uniform, von weiblichen Soldaten bei gesellschaftlichen Anlässen getragen. **G3** 'Zarengrüne' Spezialuniform der Offiziere für besondere formelle Anlässe.

H1 Dieser Mantel findet sich in verschiedenen Farbtönen von mittelgrau bis dunkelgrün. Man beachte die Verwendung unterschiedlicher Farben im Feld: Soldaten haben nur einen Mantel und finden die ständige Modifikation der Insignien mühsam. Man beachte die Kombination von AK-74/BG-15 Gewehr und Granatenwerfer. **H2** Man beachte die spezielle Arbeitsjacke mit Pelzkragen für Offiziere. **H3** Die neue Soldatenjacke, ähnlich wie H2; man beachte den RPG-18, eine neuartige 'Wegwerf'-Raketenwerferröhre.

I1 Mäntel aus Schofwolle sind unter Offizieren verbriefet und werden in arktischen Regionen bei extrem Wetterverhältnissenauch an Soldaten ausgegeben. Die *ushanka* für Offiziere ist aus echtem Pelz oder Fell gemacht. **I2** Dieser Mantel findet sich vor allem bei Offizieren der niedrigeren Ränge. Der Helm einen Panzerfahrzeugsoldaten identifiziert ihn dann als einen Offizier einer BMP-Einheit. **I3** Farbige Armbinden, aus Sicherheitsgründen jeden Tag gewechselt, werden oft mit diesem Overall getragen um Freund von Feind zu unterscheiden.

J1 VKK-3M Uniform, häufig bei der Besatzung von Flugzeugen mit Cockpits ohne vollständigen Luftdruckausgleich (z.B. die MiG-21) anzutreffen; hier mit GSh-4 · Helm getragen. **J2** Diese Uniform wird in Cockpits mit vollem Luftdrukausgleich getragen, z.B. MiG-23, Su-22 u.a., gewöhnlich mit Helmmodellen ZSh-1M oder ZSh-3 und einer KM-32 Gesichtsmaske. **J3** Arbeitsuniform für am Boden stationierte Besatzungsmitglieder bei kaltem Wetter.

K1 Fliegeruniform für kaltes Wetter, über G-Anzügen in Cockpits ohne Luftdruckausgleich und Heizung getragen. Die ZSh-3 Helm hat keine Kommunikationsverbindungen und wird über dem ledernen ShZ-61 Kommunikationshelm getragen. **K2** Notfalls über den G-Anzug getragen und auch in hellblau hergestellt. **K3** Diese Kombination ist typisch für Hubschrauberpiloten bei kaltem Wetter.

L1, L3 Zwei Möglichkeiten, den OP-1 Anzug zu tragen. Die häufigste Beschwerde bezeichnet ihn als zu heiss und anstrengend zu tragen; da er nicht hermetisch versiegelt ist, muss er über einem chemisch behandelten Stoffanzug getragen werden. Im Gegensatz zu L1 mit einer ShM Maske trägt der Offizier in L3 das ShM Maske Model K mit Sprechvorrichtung. **L2** Besser abgesicherter L-1 Anzug für chemische Aufklärungssoldaten mit besserer ShMS Maske mit optischen Glaslinsen. Diese Figuren tragen verschiedene Vergiftungsdetektoren.